MERCURY HOUSE SAN FRANCISCO

宋刻梅花喜神譜

GUIDE TO A PLUM

CAPTURING BLOSSOM

by SUNG PO-JEN

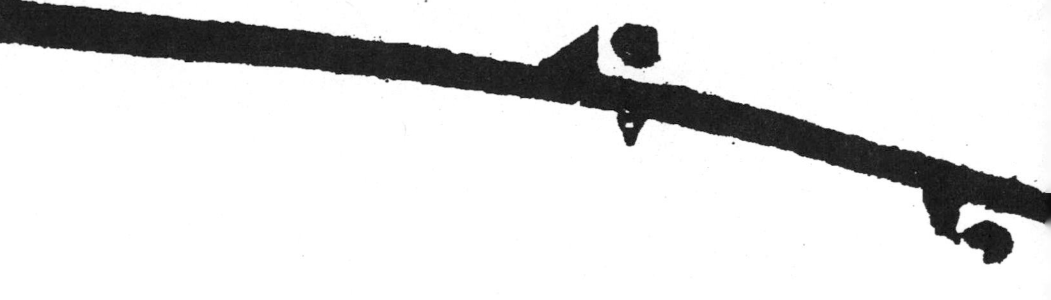

The Chinese Classic Translated
with Commentaries by Red Pine

Introduction by Lo Ch'ing

Published in the United States by Mercury House, San Francisco, California, a nonprofit publishing company devoted to the free exchange of ideas and guided by a dedication to literary values.

United States Constitution, First Amendment: Congress shall make no law respecting an establishment of religion, or prohibiting the free exercise thereof; or abridging the freedom of speech, or of the press; or the right of the people peaceably to assemble, and to petition the Government for a redress of grievances.

Printed on recycled, acid-free paper
Manufactured in the United States of America
Designed by Thomas Christensen

— *Library of Congress Cataloging-in-Publication Data* —

Sung, Po-jen.
[Mei-hua hsi-shen-p'u. English]
Guide to capturing a plum blossom / by Sung Po-jen ; translated by Red Pine ; with an introduction by Lo Ch'ing.
p. cm.
ISBN 1-56279-077-3
1. Sung, Po-jen. 2. Flowering plums in art. 3. Flowering plum—Poetry. I. Pine, Red. II. Title.
ND1049.S795A4 1995
759.951—dc20 95-18816
CIP

FIRST EDITION
5 4 3 2 1

Translator's Preface

Plum pictures and plum poems have been on my mind ever since I found Sung Po-jen's *Guide to Capturing a Plum Blossom* in China's old cultural capital of Hangchou, west of Shanghai. That was six years ago, a few days before the tanks rolled through Tienanmen in June of 1989. I was browsing through the only bookstore in Hangchou that sold old books, and I found a hand-bound copy of the 1928 edition of Sung Po-jen's *Guide* on a shelf with other dusty survivors of the Cultural Revolution. I'd never heard of Sung Po-jen or his *Guide,* but I was captivated by the pictures. I bought the book and took it back to my hotel room and tried to read the poems. I soon realized that the poetry of a thirteenth-century scholar-official was beyond my reach, which was limited to the more accessible works of Chinese Buddhists. I put the book down and a few weeks later, back in Taiwan, I gave it to my friend Lo Ch'ing. It was a fortuitous decision.

Lo Ch'ing had studied art with the last emperor's cousin, and he had heard of Sung Po-jen's *Guide,* but he had never seen a complete copy. Surprised by our good fortune, we agreed to enjoy the book together. Every Wednesday for the next four months, we sat down on his straw mats, surrounded ourselves with piles of dictionaries, dynastic histories, anthologies, and compendia of all sorts, and spent the whole morning working our way through five or six poems and as many pots of tea.

As the result of our efforts, I was able to make rough translations into English. But before I had time to polish them sufficiently for publication, I put them aside to finish work on a book about Chinese hermits, then to embark on a series of journeys in China that involved the production of more than a thousand radio programs, and finally to move back to America. It's taken me five years to pick them up again.

I regret the long delay as well as the mistakes I may have made where I have ignored Lo Ch'ing's advice and followed my own perverse interpretations. The notes, too, hardly do justice to our weekly discussions or the background Sung Po-jen expected of his readers. But the Thundercloud plum I planted last year in my garden has begun to let go of its first blossoms, and I can no longer hold onto these. In passing them on to the reader, I hope that something of their original fragrance has remained and that the pictures, reproduced from the edition of 1261, will make up for any loss of spirit.

Red Pine, Spring 1995
Port Townsend, Washington

Acknowledgments

The translator is indebted to Lo Ch'ing, Deborah Rudoph, and Paul Hansen for help with the Chinese; to Christina McLennan and Michael O'Connor for help with the English; to the Port Townsend Bakery, the Salal Cafe, Mercury House, Interwest Savings Bank, Jane and Kim Stallings, Shannon Gentry and Jack Estes, Carol and Richard Porter, Paul Hansen and Jennifer Clarke, Martin Merz and Bruce Grill, for wages, royalties, loans, and outright gifts.

for Paul Hansen

Introduction

Sung Po-jen's *Mei-hua hsi-shen-p'u,* or *Guide to Capturing a Plum Blossom,* was printed from woodblocks in 1238 and thus became the world's earliest-known printed book of art. Two decades later, a copy of the book passed into the hands of the Chinhua Shuangkueitang Publishing House, and the publisher added this short note to his 1261 edition of the book:

> Those who sing the praises of the plum flower might capture its form but not its essence. Recently, I came across this book, which not only succeeds in capturing the flower's spirit but also explores its inexhaustible forms. Reading it is like chewing sugar cane: the longer you chew, the better it tastes. Surely this is the crown of plum flower poetry.

Despite such praise, Sung's book would have been lost if a single copy of the 1261 edition had not come down to us in the following manner:

When the Mongols completed their conquest of China in 1277, the mixture of Chinese nationalism and aesthetics displayed in Sung Po-jen's *Guide* became treasonous, and his book disappeared from public notice. Although artists consulted the book in private, no one was willing to affix their name to our surviving copy until it appeared 300 years later in the collection of the sixteenth-century painter Wen Cheng-ming.

After Wen died, his copy passed through other unknown hands for another 200 years, until it surfaced in Peking's antique market, as described by the famous collector and book connoisseur Huang P'i-lieh in the colophon that he added to the book:

> At the beginning of 1801, I decided to travel north with my friends Ku Nan-ya and Hsia Fang-mi. The day we left, my friend Ch'u Mu-fu presented me with an album of plum flower paintings. I put them in my luggage thinking to ask friends along the way to add their poems on the facing pages. Shortly afterwards, my friend Ch'en Chung-yu joined us, and we sailed off together.
>
> When we arrived at Maple Bridge, my relative Yuan T'ing-t'ao

saw us off with wine and presented us with a branch of plum flowers from his courtyard to wish us good luck in the civil service examination. We took a line from the T'ang poem that goes "I have nothing to give but a branch of spring," and we all wrote poems with this as our inspiration.

After leaving, we continued on to Yangchou, where Nan-ya painted four plum flower paintings in a snowstorm, one of which depicted Shou-chieh presenting his gift, and all of which we added to Mu-fu's album. Enjoying ourselves, we titled the album *Plum Flower Words Are Perfumed Words.*

In the middle of the second month, we finally arrived in Peking and went looking for books in the Liulichang antique market. At the Wentsui Bookstore I found a Sung dynasty copy of *Guide to Capturing a Plum Blossom.* I was amazed that such a rare treasure would fall into my hands, and at the same time I was reminded of the paintings of Ch'u Mu-fu and Ku Nan-ya. It was such a coincidence, I summoned my old friends, and we met again to write poems about my new treasure.

Later, when I returned home, I failed to find Sung's book listed in the reader's guide to Ch'ien Tseng's famous collection of books. Fortunately I had also acquired a later, more complete version of Ch'ien's reader's guide, and here I found Sung's book listed. And finally I realized what a rare possession my copy of the 1261 edition was.

Recognizing the book's importance, Huang asked his relative Yuan T'ing-t'ao to trace two copies in outline form, one of which he presented to the famous scholar Juan Yuan. Juan added his own colophon to this copy and passed it on to the Ch'ing court, where it was reprinted in the collection of books known as the *Yuan-wei pieh-tsang.* Yuan T'ing-t'ao's second outline copy was also reprinted, though not until after his death, by the Kuniyuan Publishing House. In addition to spreading the book's fame through these two outline copies, Huang also had the 1261 edition reprinted in its original form in 1823 among the later collections of the Chihputsu Library. I recently came across a copy of this edition, collected earlier by Chou Tso-jen, the brother of Lu Hsun, and added it to my own collection.

In 1851 Huang's own copy of the book passed into the hands of Yu Ch'ang-sui, and Yu loaned the book to the painter Chiang Chung-li, who refused to return it. Only through trickery was Yu able to get the book back, and he added this note to its growing list of colophons: "I will never show this book to anyone who hasn't been my friend for at least ten years." Yu called it among the most precious objects in the world.

From Yu Ch'ang-sui, the book passed to P'an Tsu-yin and then to P'an Ching-shu, who inherited it in 1921 on her thirtieth birthday. P'an Ching-shu was the wife of the famous painter and collector Wu Hu-fan. The couple loved this book so much, they covered its pages with nearly fifty seals designed especially for the purpose. From P'an and Wu, the book then passed into the collection of the Shanghai Museum, which reprinted it in 1981 and thus made the world's oldest-known printed book of art available for our use.

About the book's author, we know next to nothing. According to the brief biography included in Huang P'i-lieh's colophon, Sung Po-jen was a native of the Huchou area of Chekiang province. His personal name was Ch'i-chih, and his pen name was Hsueh-yen, both of which had patriotic echoes in Chinese. After passing the poetry section of the civil service examination, he was appointed to supervise the salt trade in Huaiyang along the Grand Canal. This is all we know of the man, except for the few personal notes he slipped into another collection of ninety-odd poems that survive in the *Ssu-k'u ch'uan-shu.*

Although we have no dates for his birth or death, we know Sung lived in southern China in the first half of the thirteenth century, when the northern part of China was in the hands of the nomadic Jurchens, who were, themselves, about to lose the north to the Mongols. Sung wanted to do something to encourage his countrymen to recover the north, and he expressed his frustration and patriotic feelings in his verse, which he likened to withered leaves teasing the wind and dried-up lotus leaves battered by the rain. And so he published his book, with its image of the flower that blooms in the middle of winter and with its poems that recall the glories of China's past. In this Sung was not alone. During this period Chinese intellectuals turned to their culture's ancient roots for inspiration and solace in the face of disunion and exile. In painting and poetry, they chose the flowering plum as their symbol.

In his own preface, Sung Po-jen had this to say:

I am so addicted to plum blossoms that I laid out my garden around them and built a pavilion to view them and published a collection of poems called *The Pure and Fragile* in praise of them. And still I failed to exhaust their subtlety, much like my ancestor Sung Ching, who turned to writing about clouds when plum blossoms proved too elusive.

When their flowers are in bloom, my heart is filled with the purest snow and my body is buried beneath clouded moonlight. I never tire of lingering beside a bamboo fence or a thatched hut to smell their stamens, to breathe on their petals and inhale their fragrance, and to taste their pollen. I enjoy the sight of plum blossoms whether they are facing up or down or are open or folded.

Detached, refined, and rare, beyond the world of red dust, so different from the Two Gentlemen of Kuchu, the Four Worthies of Shangshan, the Six Eccentrics of Chuhsi, the Eight Immortals of Wine, the Nine Elders of Loyang, or the Eighteen Erudites of Yingchou, they float beyond the confines of form and the mundane world of man, and beyond the rhapsodies written on such flowers as the peach blossom or peony.

Thus, I painted the flower from the unfolding of its buds to the falling of its petals. I painted more than 200 portraits, and after eliminating those that were too staid or too frail, I was left with 100 distinct views. And to each I added an old-style poem and titled the result *Guide to Capturing a Plum Blossom.* Actually, though, it's about capturing the spirit of the plum blossom. And while there are also guides that describe peonies, chrysanthemums, and bamboo, this is not the same kind of guide. I have published it in the hope of sharing it with other lovers of plum flowers.

In devoting my time to such an insignificant task, how, someone might ask, can this be of any use to the world? Might not these pages end up as lids on someone's jars and jugs? Despite such a possibility, surely there are like-minded people who would enjoy turning a few pages when the flowers aren't yet in bloom, people who would prefer to fill their imaginations with the beauty of a single branch on a deserted hillside or the desolation of

Yangchou before spring, people who can't let a day pass without seeing plum flowers, people who could spend their lives thinking about plum flowers. I have not painted plum flowers for the sake of painting plum flowers. In this, the artistry of Abbot Chung-jen and Yang Wu-chiu are quite beyond my ability.

Someone also joked, "When this flower's whiteness and perfume are gone, it can stop the thirst of armies with its red and yellow fruit and blend the perfect soup in the tripod of the state. This book of yours should likewise move loyal and patriotic readers to act the part of generals in the field or ministers at court in straightening their sashes and jade scepters and in bringing peace to the kingdom. But by focusing instead on the aesthetic beauty of a half-hidden tree in a garden after a snowfall or a branch reaching beyond a bamboo fence reflected in the water, you have concerned yourself with frozen verse and forgotten the root while chasing among twigs."

I rose and thanked him, "And that's why I have a poem about tripods and soup at the end of my *Guide*." My friend clapped his hands and smiled, "In that case, your *Guide* is not in vain. It cannot be called insignificant or of no use to the world, and it should be spread as widely as possible so that it might be passed on to future generations."

Fortunately for Sung, his book appeared just as the technology of printing that began with Buddhist sutras in the ninth century was extended to works of literature and art in the twelfth and thirteenth centuries. This technological revolution also brought with it a new attitude toward knowledge. Until the Sung dynasty, books were the private possessions of those able to afford laboriously produced handwritten copies. The use of woodblocks and movable type suddenly made knowledge reproducible and available in the marketplace. Ideas that were once the preserve of a small elite were now exchanged as easily as other merchandise.

This marked the second of the three stages through which Chinese culture has passed—the first being the invention of writing, the second being the development of printing, and the third being the introduction of personal computers. With the advent of printing, books were produced in great numbers, and private collectors emerged. Intellectuals now had easy access to a wide range of materials on Confucianism, Taoism, and Buddhism that was beyond any one person's capacity to memorize, and the publishing centers that developed provided a fertile ground for a new synthesis of ideas that resulted in what Western scholars have called Neo-Confucianism.

Turning their backs on the traditional approach to the derivation of knowledge from discursive thought, Neo-Confucians held that the secrets of Nature could be discovered only through the investigation of things. Painters, too, followed this early scientific approach. And they developed a complicated grammar of painting, as they tried to represent natural forms and landscapes in a seemingly realistic manner.

Realism, though, was not what the Sung painters were after. They were after the essence of things. The great poet and calligrapher Su Tung-p'o warned his colleagues, however, against a one-sided search for this essence. He held up the works of Wang Wei, whose paintings, he said, contained poems and whose poems contained paintings, as examples of a more balanced approach. Su maintained that the ultimate goal of both painting and poetry was to express one's feelings and ideas. The creation of a likeness or a verbal cliché was not the goal of art. The goal was to express meaning beyond words and feeling beyond representations, and thus to encourage painters to paint like poets and poets to write like painters.

From the late Northern Sung (960–1127) to the Southern Sung (1127–1276) dynasties, we begin to see scattered examples of this effort to combine poetry and painting, in which a poem is not merely an annotation to a painting and a painting is not simply an illustration of a poem. Though they might overlap, poetry and painting were seen as each maintaining its own integrity. In this respect, Sung Po-jen's book was the first—and the last—attempt to put Su Tung-p'o's theory into practice on a large scale. It was not only the world's first book of art, but also the first book that combined painting and poetry.

Sung's book is also significant because it attempts to fathom the essence of a material object through detailed, empirical examination and uses the results of that examination to form the basis for that object's deconstruction and reconstruction on a different plane. Once the reader has the flower's 100 stages memorized, he has the key to the plum flower and the key to Nature as well. With this key he can create his own plum flower universe without having to observe Nature at all. Later painters who wanted to paint plum flowers were encouraged to follow the book rather than Nature. How, they asked, could anyone hope to observe the plum flower as meticulously as Sung Po-jen? This, then, was also the first example of postmodernism in the history of Chinese painting. In Sung's book, form becomes a catalyst for meaning, and conversely, meaning conjures up form.

The sudden appearance of this book was unprecedented and represented a climax that has yet to be surpassed. Sung Po-jen's *Guide to Capturing a Plum Blossom* is a most remarkable book indeed, and its flowers are as fresh today as they were over 750 years ago. Breathe in their fragrance, and see for yourself.

Lo Ch'ing, April 1995
Taipei, Taiwan

First Buds

Four Branches

I *Wheat Eyes*

a southern branch erupts with buds
unmarked means a year of plenty
Han Kuang-wu comes to mind
restoring the throne with a meal

A southern branch feels the warmth of spring before other branches. The Chinese still look to the plum tree for the first sign of spring, and they examine its buds to predict the coming season of growth. It was from such buds that the career of Emperor Kuang-wu began. The year he was born, nine ears appeared on a single stalk of corn in his district, and his mother named him Hsiu, meaning "grain flower." Later, when he was put in charge of a granary, he sold wheat and millet at discounted prices and gained a large following among the oppressed. In A.D. 25 he toppled the usurper Wang Mang, restored the Han dynasty, and ascended the throne as Emperor Kuang-wu.

Throughout his book, Sung Po-jen uses variant forms of characters, as if he were testing his readers' erudition as well as their patience. In the second line, for example, he uses the name of Mount Kungtung in place of two similar characters that mean "blank" or "unmarked." Puns are also fair game: "meal" is a homophone for "revolution."

梅花喜神譜卷上　　雪岩

蓓蕾四枝

麥眼

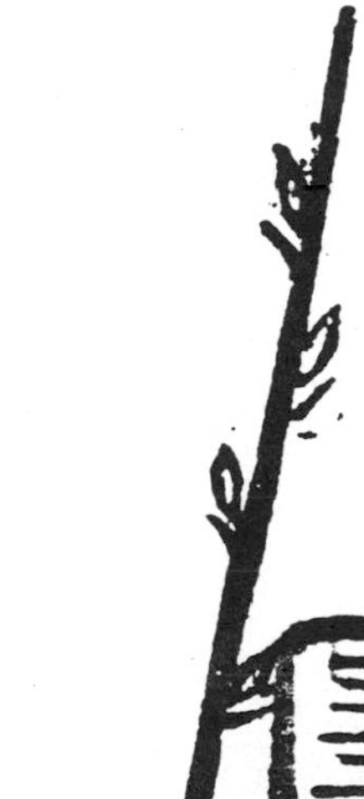

南枝發岐穎　崆峒占歲登

當思漢光武　一飯能中興

2 *Willow Eyes*

silently watching the Sui Dike procession
the glories the endless failures
willows don't bend to look pretty
what they see isn't commonplace

In A.D. 605 Emperor Yang of the Sui dynasty toured the newly completed Grand Canal in a procession of boats that stretched for 100 kilometers. To provide a shaded promenade and to guard against erosion, the emperor had willows planted along the dikes. Later, the dynasty's name was applied to new sections of this important trade route that linked the Yangtze with the Yellow River. The willow's hanging catkins remind the Chinese of a woman bending at the waist, and "willow lane" is their euphemism for a brothel-lined street. Here, though, willow eyes, like the eyes of a buddha, see through illusory form and superficial beauty. A poem by the ninth-century poet Yuan Chen includes the line: "Where does spring appear first / spring appears in the willow eyes."

柳眼

靜看隋堤人　紛紛幾榮辱

蠻腰休逞妍　所見元非俗

3 *Pepper* Eyes

lavishing poems on the first spring dawn
prayers for a thousand years
conquering winter defying old age
outlasting the ice and snow

Black pepper arrived in China in ancient times as a trade good from Southeast Asia. In addition to its use as an incense in calling down ancestral spirits, pepper was infused in alcohol to warm the extremities and offered to family elders on the first day of the new year along with poems wishing them long life. The Chinese add another year to their age on New Year's Day, rather than on their birthday.

椒眼

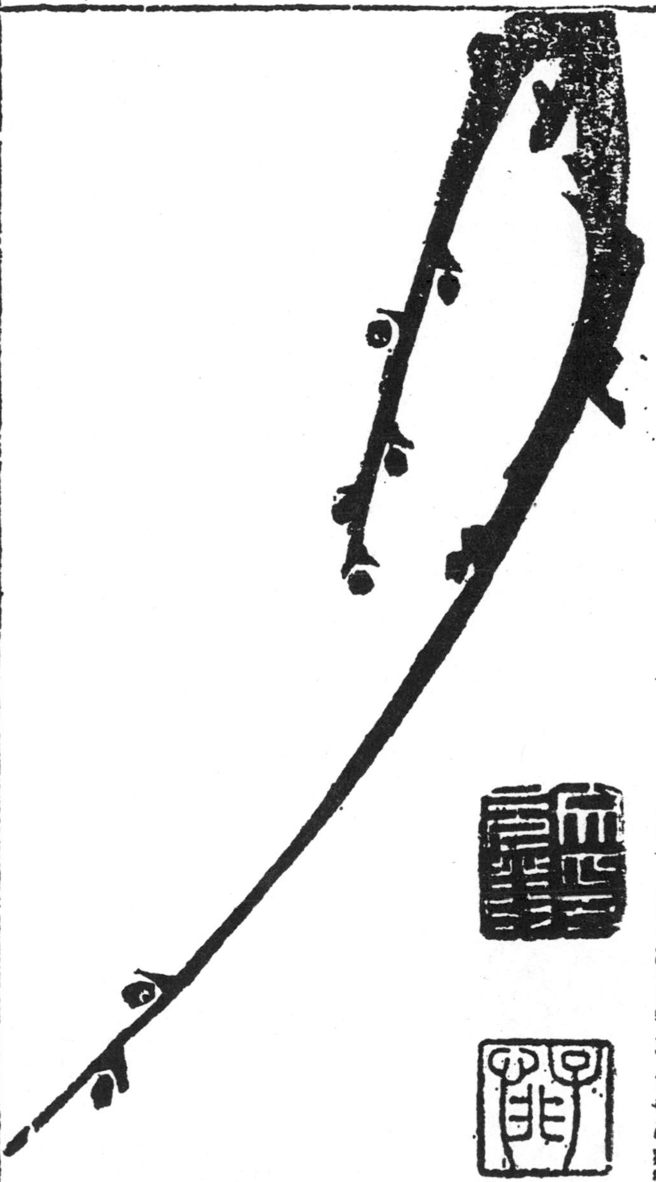

獻頌後春朝　争期千歲壽

凌寒傲歲時　自與冰霜久

4 *Crab* Eyes

scuttling across sands of rivers and seas
at home in the foulest wind and waves
preferring the Lord of the East
public death to the cauldron

Chinese tea aficionados refer to the appearance of bubbles in their kettles as the eleventh-century poet Su Tung-p'o did in a poem about brewing tea: "After the crab eyes, the fish eyes appear." "Rivers and seas" is a metaphor for the world, and "wind and waves" refers to the vicissitudes of life. The Lord of the East is the spirit of the sun and of spring. In China, crab catchers traditionally operate at night using torches. The last lines suggest the crab would rather die on a sunny beach before the eyes of its fellow creatures than by human hands.

蠏眼

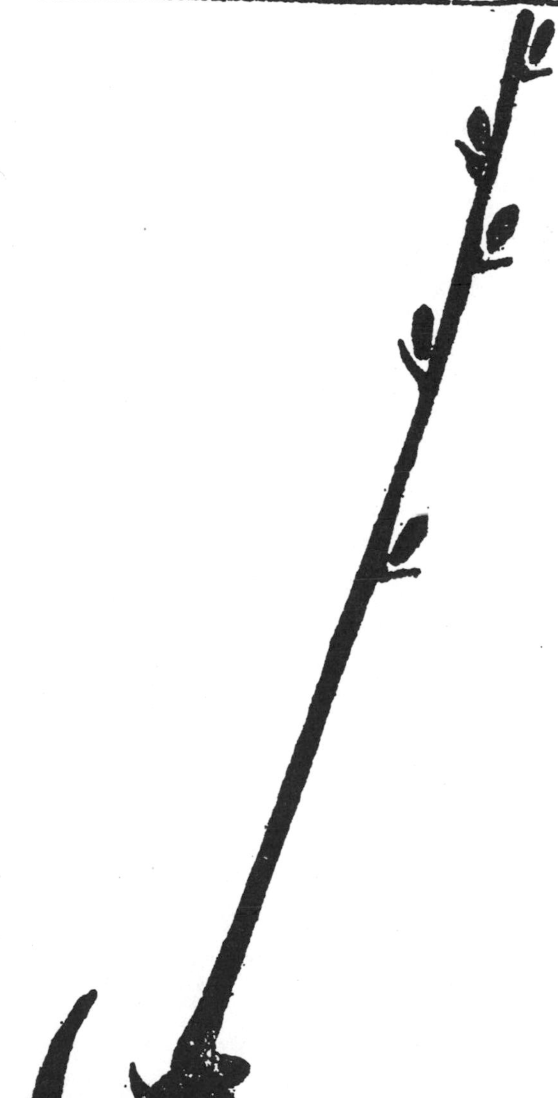

爬沙走江海　慣識風波惡

東君爲主張　顯戮逃砧鑊

Small Petals

Sixteen Branches

5 *Cloves*

herbs that warm and cool are prized
so why this fire and spice
ignoring the cinnamon's lead
destined to make things hot

Cinnamon is an important ingredient in herbal tonics designed to revitalize the body without overstimulating it. As such, its effects are described as both warming and cooling, and its application in Chinese medicine is extensive. The major use of cloves is in treating "cold" illnesses that require something hotter than cinnamon. The Chinese view illness as an imbalance between *yin* and *yang,* cold and hot. Treatment aims to restore the balance. Like pepper, cinnamon and cloves first entered China as trade goods from Southeast Asia and India.

丁香

小葉一十六枝

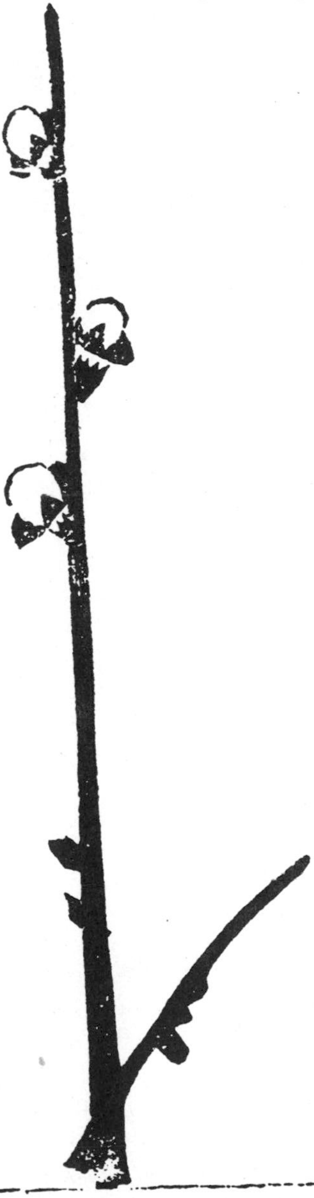

藥性貴溫涼 胡爲辛且烈

無與桂附徒 天資更趍熱

6 *Cherry*

Fan Su was lovely and sang
what more could Le-t'ien desire
to gain the emperor's favor
to shine in the Hall of Light

In 824 the lyric poet Pai Chu-yi (also known as Pai Le-t'ien) added two girls to his household staff. One of them was Fan-su, whose lips he likened to a cherry. Although he served as governor of several important prefectures south of the Yangtze, Pai was critical of government policies and failed to gain the emperor's favor. The Hall of Light was a name for the inner part of the palace that was lit day and night by the reflections from beaded curtains of gold and jade.

櫻桃

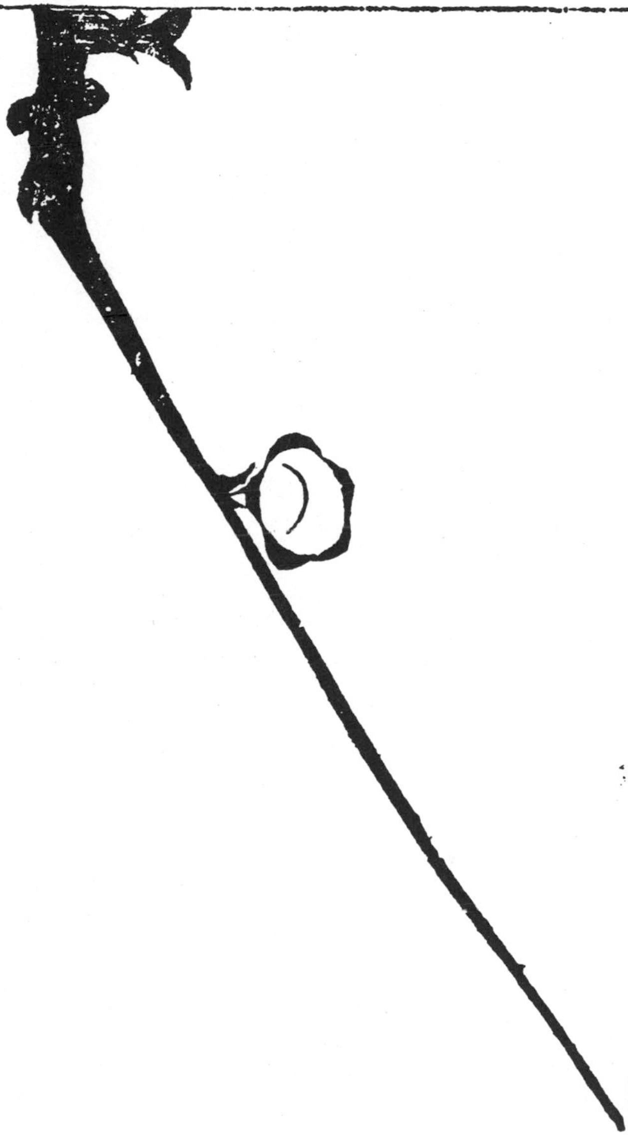

樊素艷而歌　樂天何所羨

須結帝王知　拜寵明光殿

7 *Old Man Star*

wind blows apart a rainbow of clouds
a bright star shines due south
auspicious sign for the throne
good fortune for these eyes too

The Old Man Star is Canopus, the second brightest star in the sky after Sirius. It is, however, a southern circumpolar star and only briefly visible in central China immediately after the beginning of the Lunar New Year. Its appearance during the Spring Festival has caused it to be associated with renewal and long life, and anyone who sees it is said to have an extra year added to their life. Since the emperor was acknowledged as the Son of Heaven, all celestial phenomena had a possible bearing on his reign. Not only the presence of certain stars or planets, but the appearance of certain colors was interpreted as forecasting more than the coming weather. The simultaneous appearance of the whole spectrum was considered the most auspicious of all.

老人星

風掣五雲開　明星燦南極

嘉祥自朝廷　何幸愚親識

8 *The Buddha's Crown Jewel*

the Buddha possesses a crown of light
more precious than offspring of oysters
meant to pity poor mortals
wasting their money on jewels

Buddhas are characterized as possessing a number of attributes. A protrusion on top of the head represents the attainment of supreme wisdom through meditation. Despite its radiance, this attribute is only visible to those to whom a buddha transmits his highest teaching, his crown jewel. As for pearls, the Chinese once thought they were the offspring of oysters and moonlight.

佛頂珠

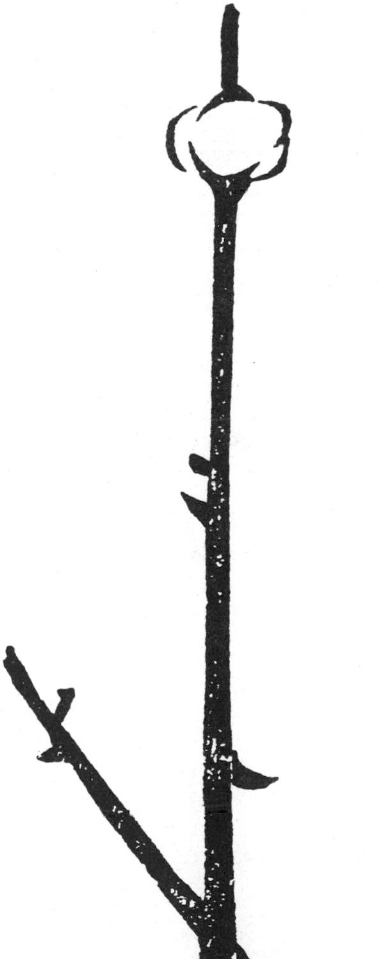

佛有光明臺　蚌胎奚足貴
聊以矜俗人　徒爲寶所貴

9 *Ancient Coin*

what the hell is that stuff
rotten cords are so disgraceful
one thing fills an empty purse
the ages value honesty

The third-century official Wang Yen was known for his vanity and precocious use of words. He was so careful to avoid the appearance of corruption that he refused to use the word "money" and called it "that stuff" instead. Sung Po-jen responds to Wang Yen's colloquial usage with one of his own. Until the beginning of the twentieth century, most Chinese coins had a hole in the middle that allowed them to be strung together into larger denominations. Rotten cords suggest unused coins, hence, excessive wealth.

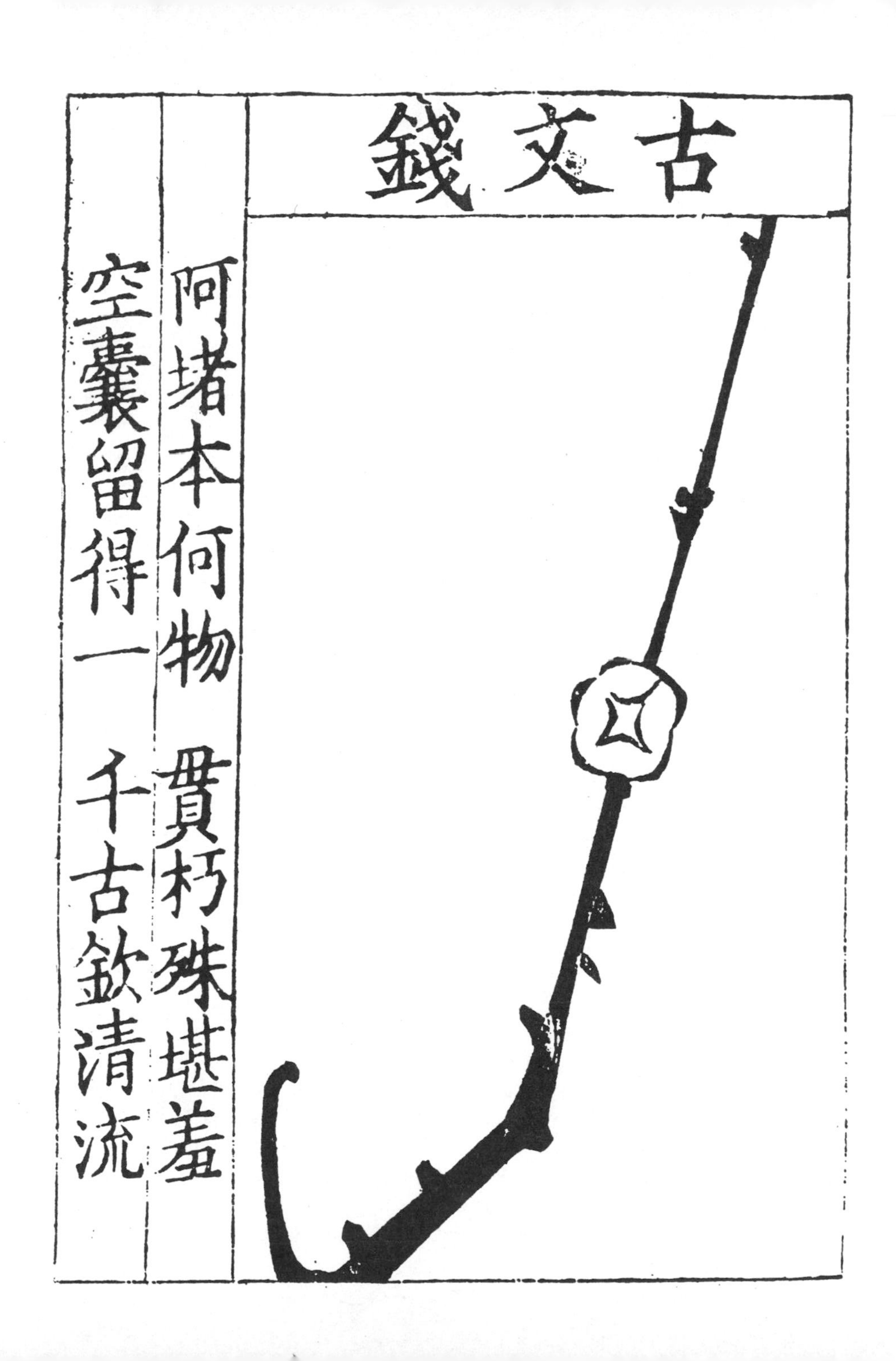
古文錢
阿堵本何物　貫朽殊堪羞
空囊留得一　千古欽清流

10 *Old Pao's Eyebrows*

dancing deftly on the stage
seductive yet demure
he bewitches all who look
Young Kuo never smiles

Early Chinese drama consisted largely of slapstick sketches involving two characters: a fool and a knave. Among such pairs were Old Pao and Young Kuo. One of their routines has Young Kuo dancing and Old Pao making fun of the length of his sleeves. When it's Old Pao's turn, his sleeves turn out to be even longer, eliciting laughter from the audience but disdain from Young Kuo. Old Pao then outdoes Young Kuo again with an even greater frown.

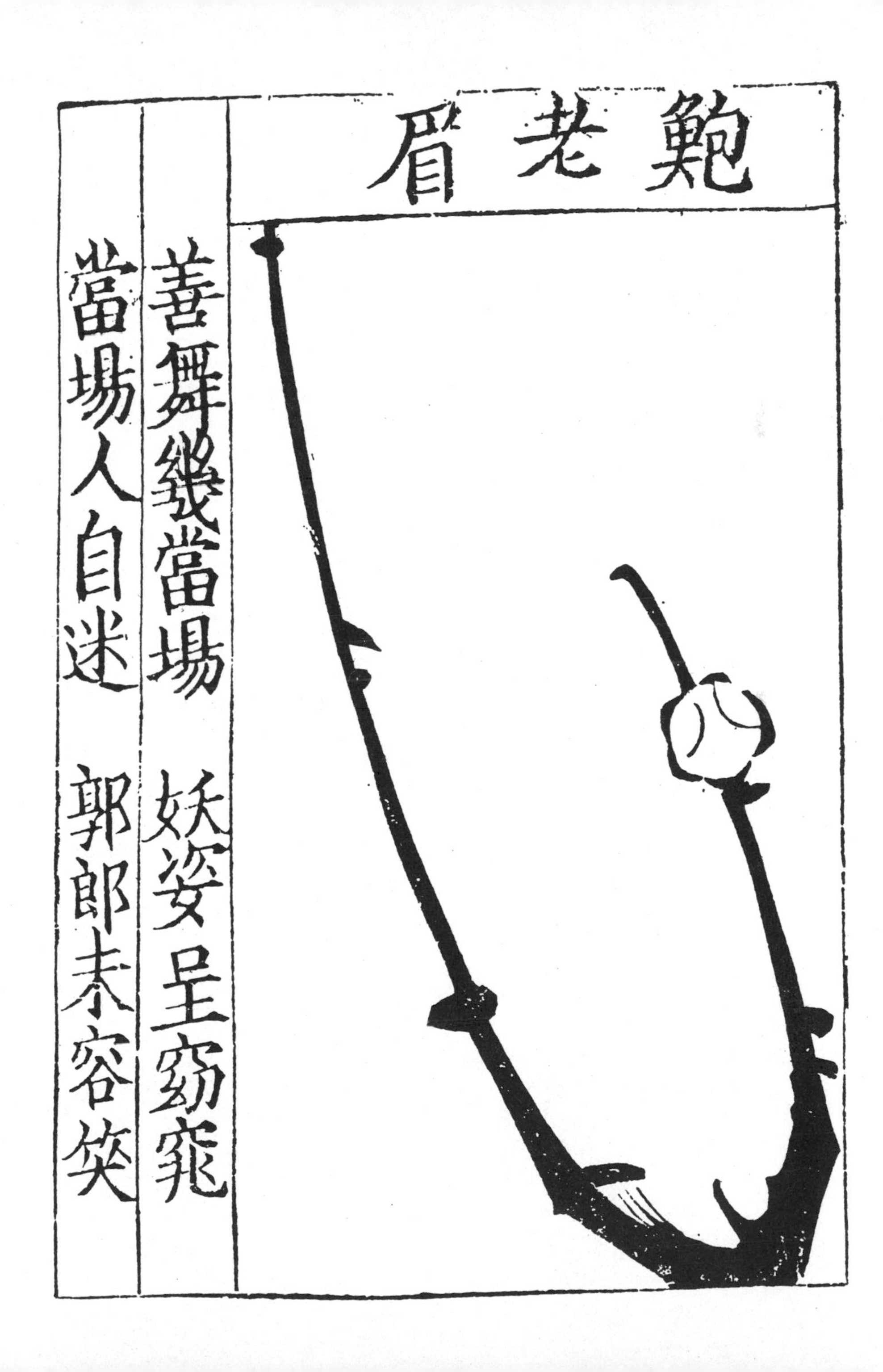
鮑老眉
善舞幾當場　妖姿呈窈窕
當場人自迷　郭郎未容笑

11 *Rabbit Lips*

you don't need to dig three holes
faithful friend of Meng T'ien
you know every book by heart
if the hand had style

A smart rabbit is said to have three holes. While Meng T'ien was completing the Great Wall in the third century B.C., he often hunted rabbits. He is said to have invented the Chinese writing brush by tying rabbit hair to a piece of bamboo. The traditional attribution notwithstanding, a brush of this description was recently unearthed in the tomb of a man buried several hundred years earlier. Until woodblock printing became popular in the thirteenth century, books were copied out by hand, and a book was often judged on the basis of its calligraphy as well as its content.

兔唇

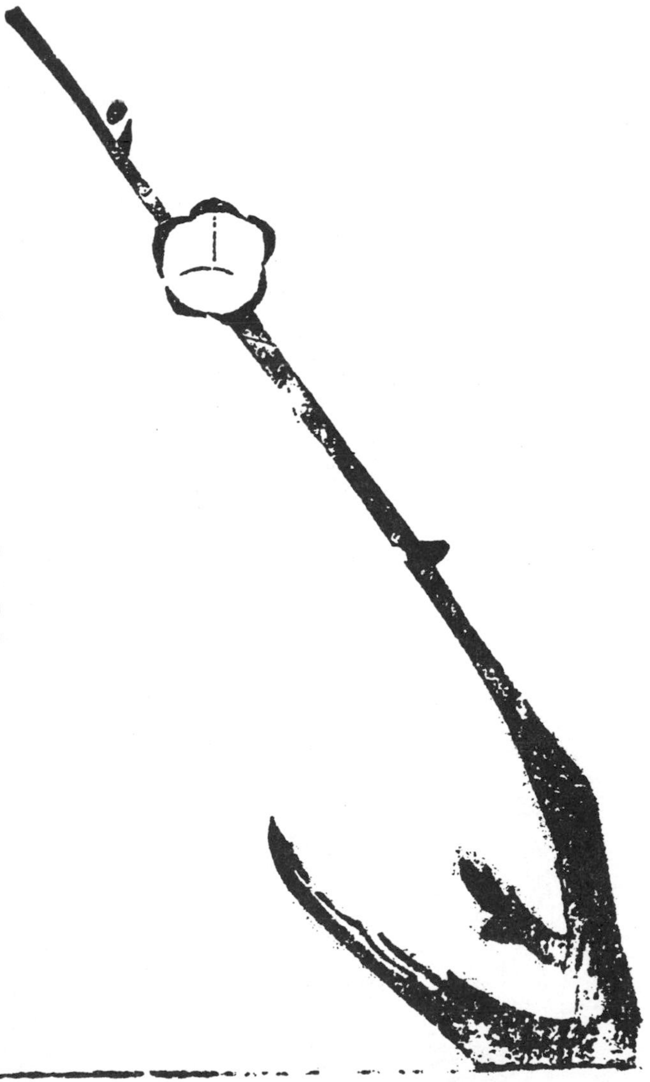

三窟不須營　蒙恬素心友

識盡天下書　只要文章手

12 *Tiger Tracks*

winter wind bends dry grass
flicks its tail along the ridge
fearful force on the loose
don't try to braid old whiskers

The Chinese liken the north wind that blows down from Siberia in winter to a roaring tiger. China is home to both the Siberian and the South China tigers. While both are on the verge of extinction, the smaller South China tiger still appears as far north as the Chungnan Mountains, where hermits have shown me their tracks. When Marco Polo visited China in the thirteenth century, he reported that tigers were so numerous in the southern parts of the empire that traveling alone was dangerous.

虎跡

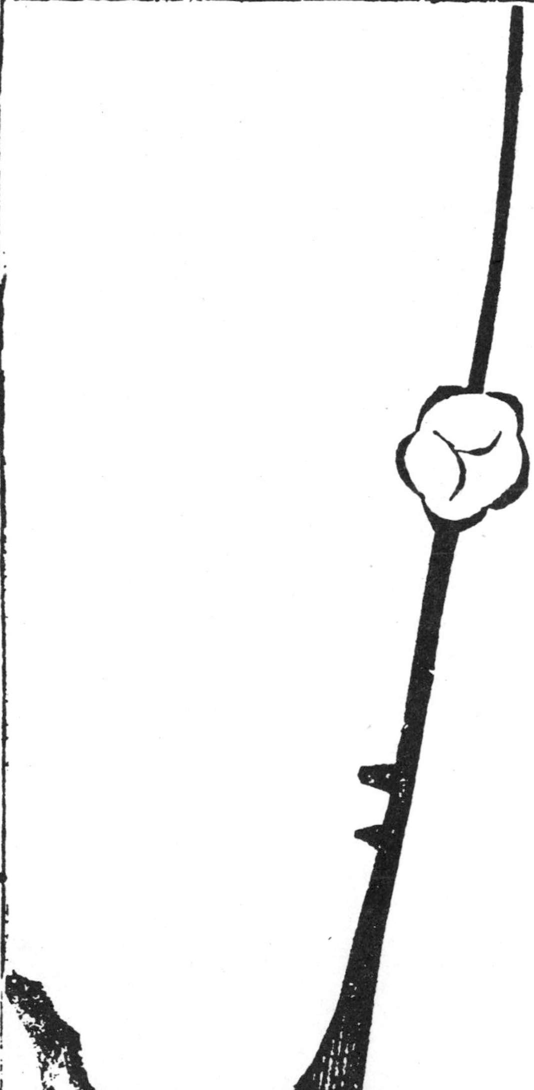

寒風偃枯草　掉尾來山巔

出柙勢可畏　老鬚寧易編

13 *Pomegranate*

brocade purse filled with pearls
nourished by a southern wind
long ago Old Tung-p'o
used it for a writing brush

The pomegranate is not native to China. It was first introduced in the second century B.C. from the central Asian kingdom of Parthia by the Chinese emissary Chang Ch'ien. The Chinese have long since used pomegranates as a symbol for the womb and its seeds to represent many sons. And they compare the south wind that ushers in another cycle of growth in early summer to the kindness parents bestow on their children. The eleventh-century poet and calligrapher Su Tung-p'o once visited a hermit so poor he didn't have a writing brush. Undeterred, Su wrote down a poem with the rind of a pomegranate.

石榴

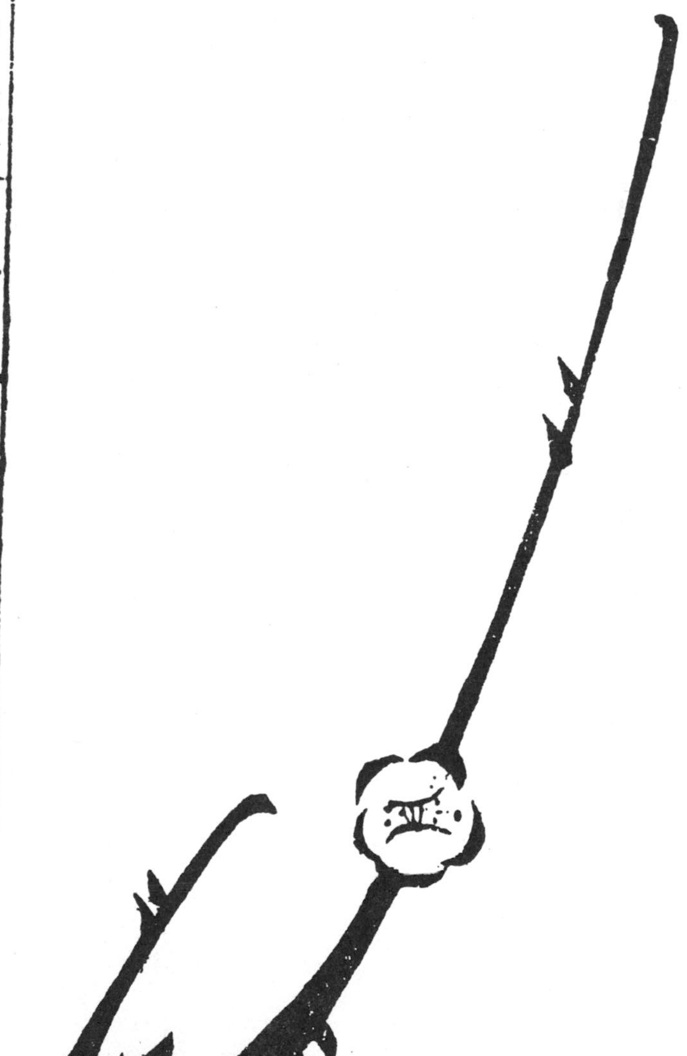

錦囊蘊珠璣　長養南風力

當年東老家　曾代中書筆

14 *Arrowhead*

growing from the mud and mire
not known for its stalk or shoots
placed upon an altar tray
the peer of pears and chestnuts

Arrowhead (*Sagittaria sagittifolia*) is an aquatic plant with long, arrow-shaped leaves. The white-fleshed tubers that grow from its roots are eaten and also used for offerings. In China, white is associated with purity and the spiritual world. Hence, white-fleshed fruits are considered superior for offerings to ancestors.

茈菰

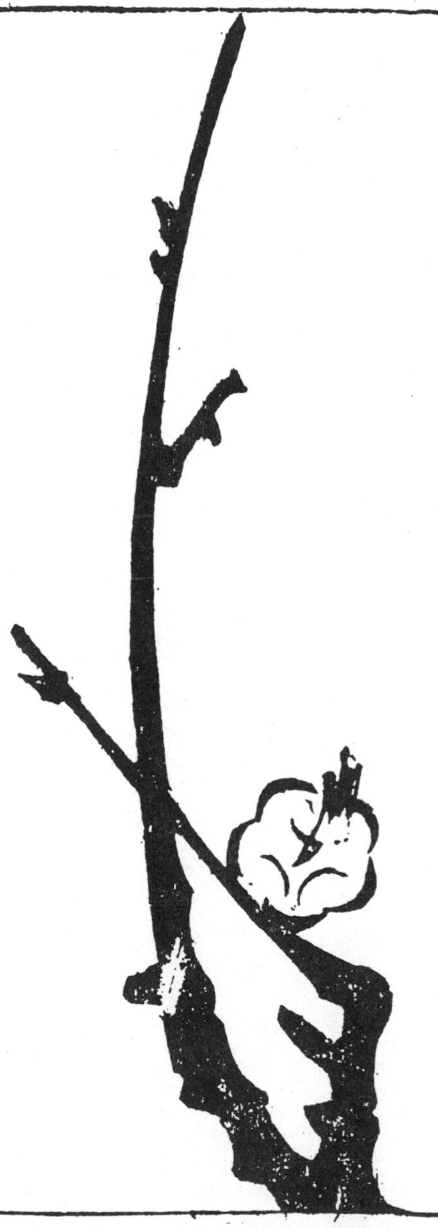

來自淤泥中　根苗何足取
闘飣上盤登　敢為梨栗伍

15 *Quince Heart*

Wanling has a sacred root
round and red a jewel-like fruit
when the state of Wei thanked Ch'i
crimson jade was token payment

The quince (*Chaenomeles sinensis*) is a sour apple-like fruit that ranges from red to yellow in color. A poem in the *Book of Songs* titled "Quince Heart" was written nearly 3,000 years ago to thank Duke Hsuan of the state of Ch'i for coming to the aid of the state of Wei. It begins: "You gave us a quince / we return crimson jade / not to repay you / to deepen our friendship." "*Ling-ken*:sacred-root" refers to the tongue as well as to the ancestor of a state, but I have yet to discover why Sung Po-jen finds it in Wanling or what Wanling has to do with the quince. Wanling was the ancient capital of what is now Anhui province and more than 700 kilometers south of the ancient states of Ch'i and Wei. It was also the home of the eleventh-century poets Mei Yao-ch'en and Hsieh Ching-ch'u. Hsieh's ancestor Hsieh T'iao also served as the province's governor and was one of the greatest poets of the fifth century. Perhaps Sung felt a poetic debt to one or more of these men. Mei Yao-ch'en was called The Gentleman of Wanling and was responsible, along with Ou-yang Hsiu, for initiating a period of realism in Chinese literature.

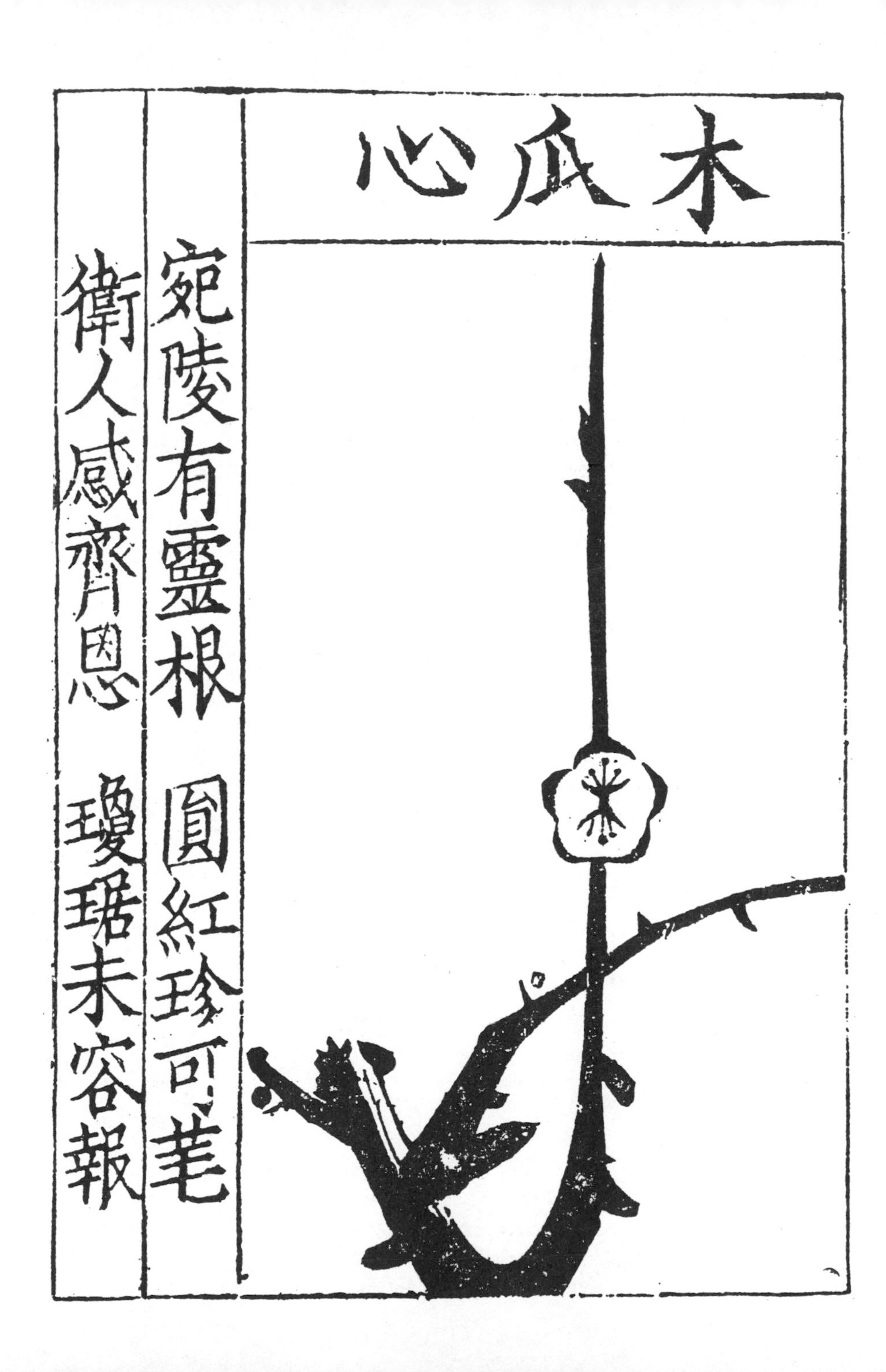
木瓜心
宛陵有靈根 圓紅珍可芼
衛人感齊恩 瓊琚未容報

16 *Babyface*

when their brocade wrap comes off
children look so cute
when they act like ghosts
our love soon turns to fear

Chinese mothers still carry their babies on their backs, wrapped in blankets tied across their chests. An embroidered blanket suggests the child of a well-to-do family. Here the "brocade wrap" also refers to the perianth, or outer covering of the plum blossom, which has just fallen off to reveal the petals before they have had a chance to unfold.

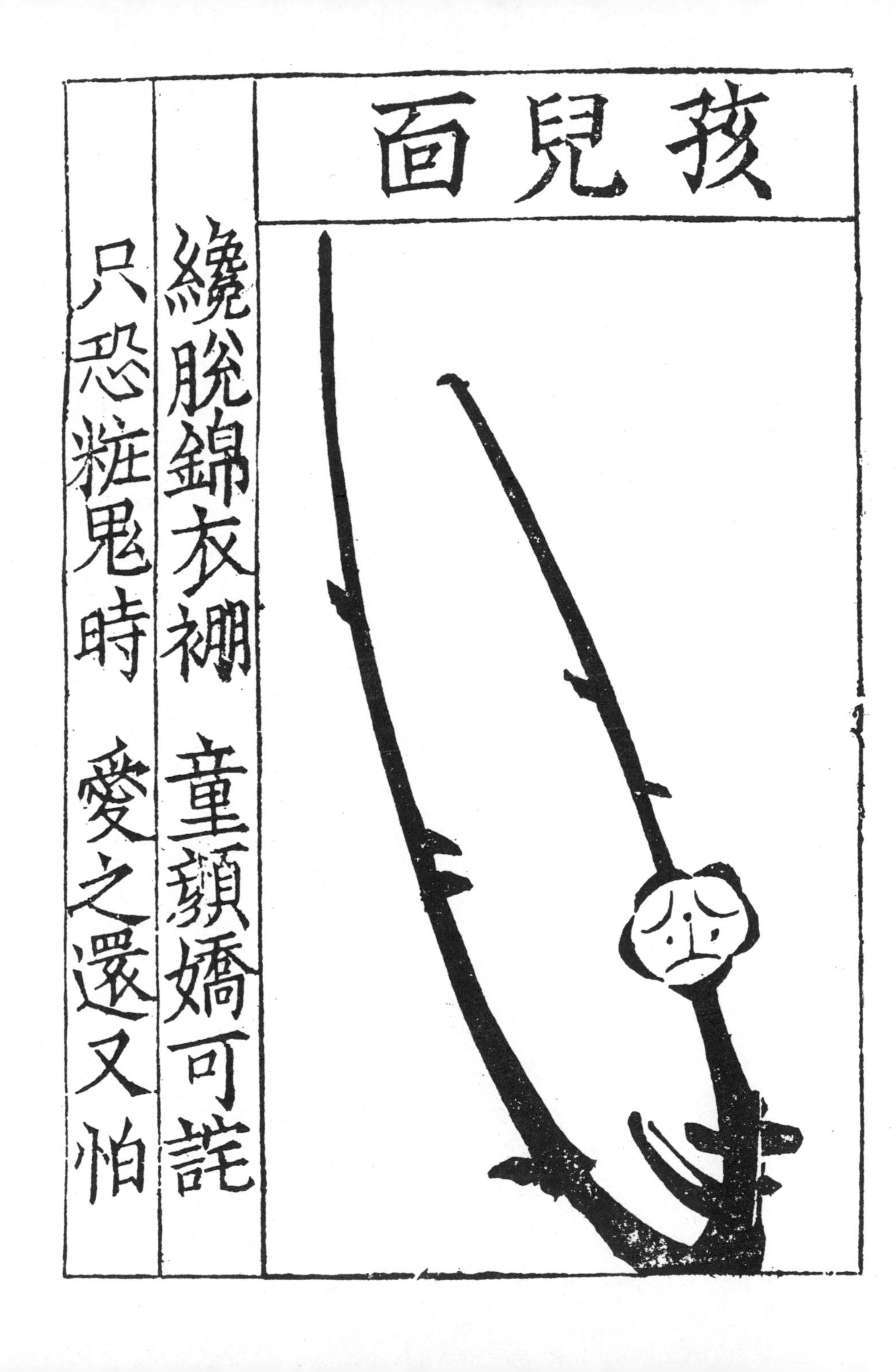
孩兒面
纔脫錦衣繃　童顏嬌可詫
只恐粧鬼時　愛之還又怕

17 *Plum*

where it hangs above a well
travelers dare not touch their hats
beside a road it grows in vain
who looks at it with pleasure

Once when Ch'en Chung-tzu was living in the Wuling hills, he didn't eat for three days and lost the ability to see or hear. Above his well there was a plum tree whose fruit was half-eaten by worms. Ch'en crawled over to it, ate three mouthfuls, and soon recovered (*Mencius,* 3.2). The second line paraphrases Ts'ao Chih's "Ballad of a Gentleman," which begins: "A gentleman takes precautions / he doesn't stay where suspicion reigns / or tie his shoe in melon fields / or adjust his hat beneath plum trees." The Chinese plum is especially sour, and here it reminds travelers of their thirst.

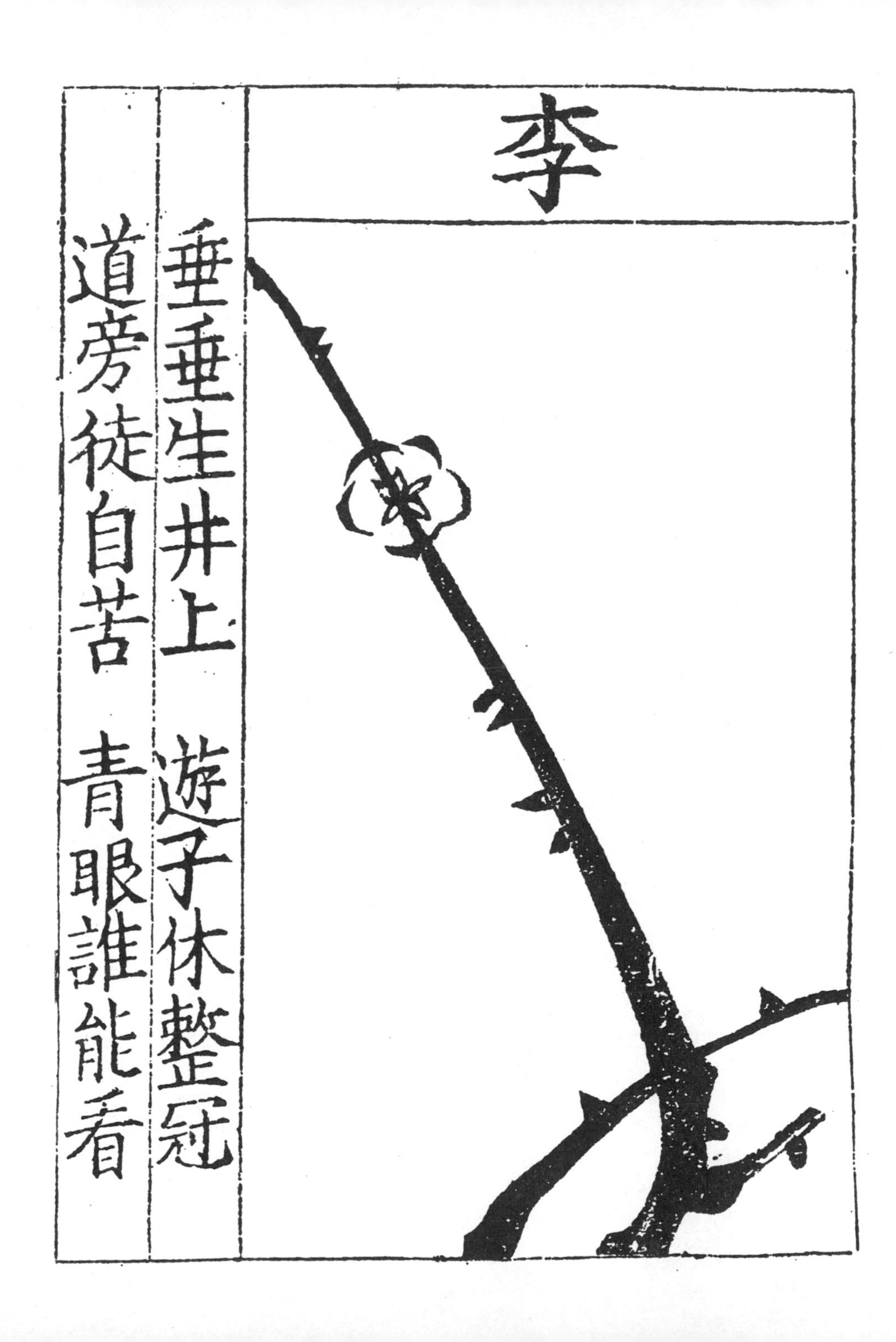
李
垂垂生井上　遊子休整冠
道旁徒自苦　青眼誰能看

18 *Melon*

Old Tungling has joined the gods
into darkness sunlight fades
shameless quest for wealth and fame
always asking for a sign

During the Ch'in dynasty, Shao P'ing was enfeoffed as the marquis of Tungling. When the Han dynasty replaced the Ch'in in 207 B.C., Shao P'ing's status was reduced to that of a commoner, and he supported himself by growing melons near his former estate east of Ch'ang-an. Ever since then, his name has been synonymous with indifference to worldly attainments. The last line suggests impatience for advancement or success.

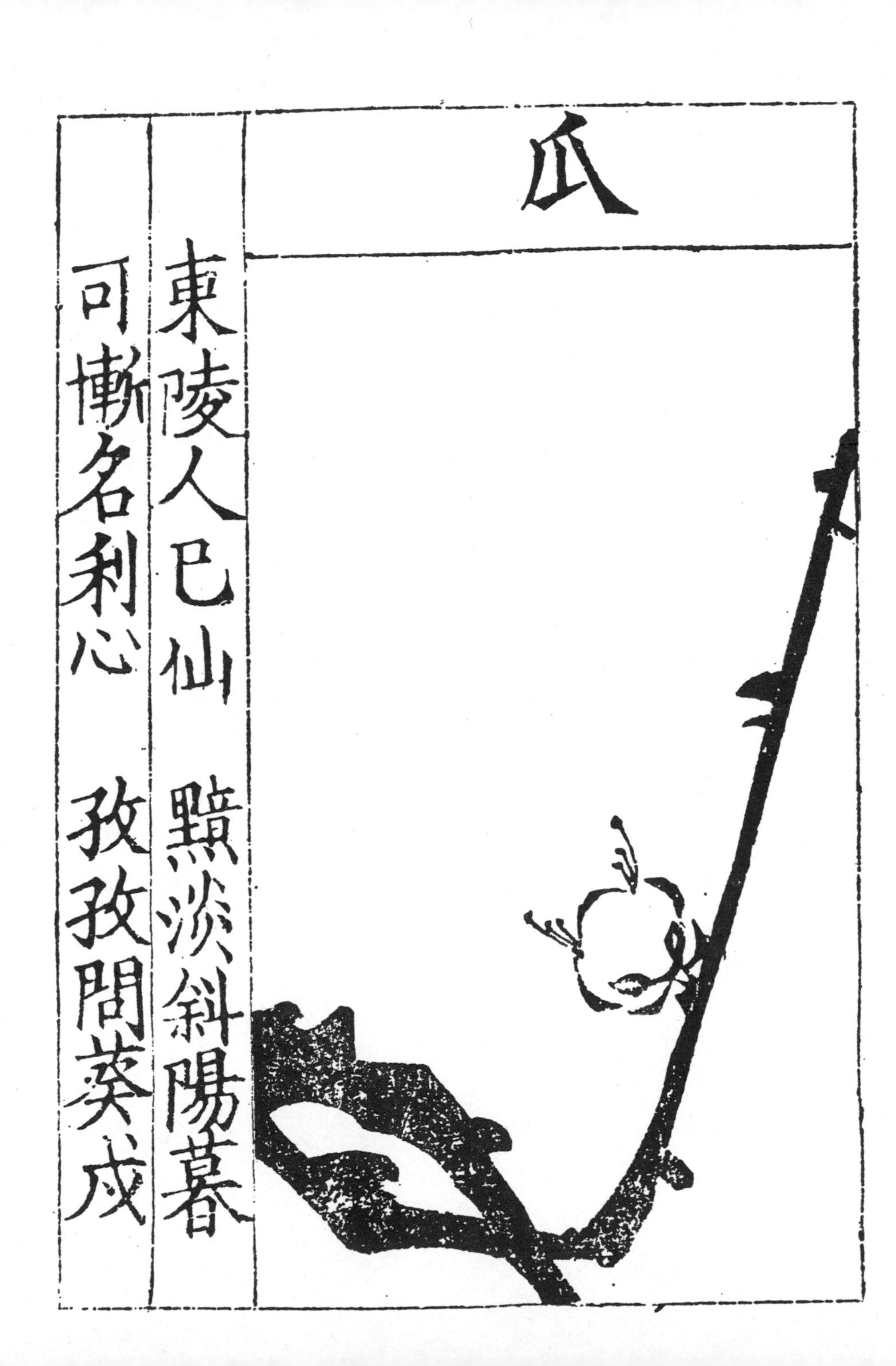

瓜
東陵人已仙　黯淡斜陽暮
可㦓名利心　孜孜問葵戍

19 *Conch Shell*

born beneath the ocean waves
brought by net to a scholar's study
vines of Yen all spread flat
where's the beam-sized brush

Chinese intellectuals have long appreciated and enjoyed writing about the unusual. Here, a scholar looks for the biggest brush he can find to praise a seashell from the Indian Ocean with as much hyperbole as he can muster. Among the many kinds of paper used in ancient China, the paper made from rattan vines that grew along Chekiang's Yen River was especially prized and reserved for special occasions.

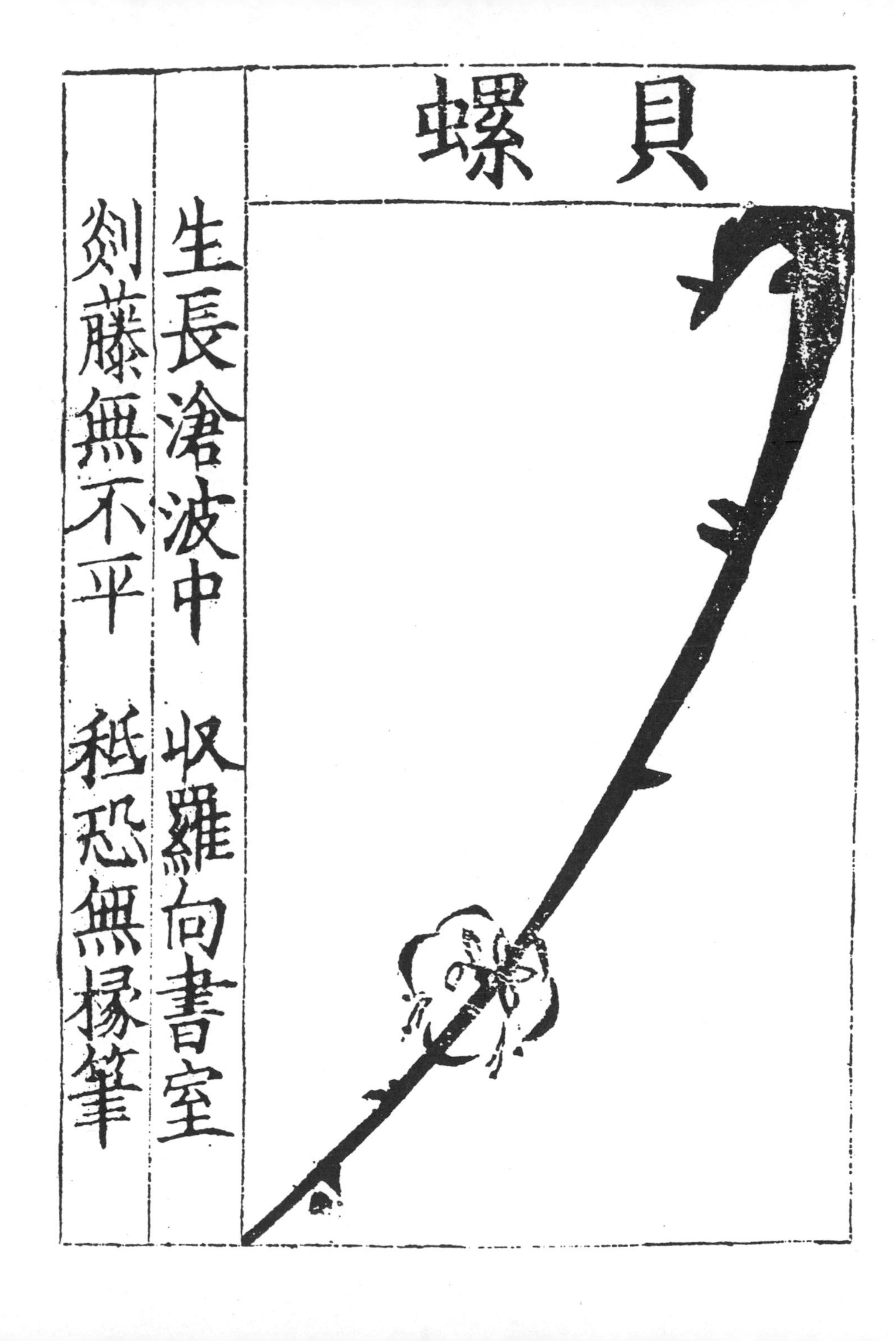
貝螺
生長滄波中　收羅向書室
剡藤無不平　秖恐無椽筆

20 *Tadpole*

polliwogs in crystal water
ancient writing looked like this
out of use since ages past
no one knows its meaning

Among the means of writing used by the early Chinese more than 3,000 years ago was a bamboo stylus that they dipped in black lacquer. In contrast to the more angular characters carved during the same period on metal and bone, these early written forms consisted of black drops and squiggly lines. They continue to require considerable effort to decipher whenever they come to light.

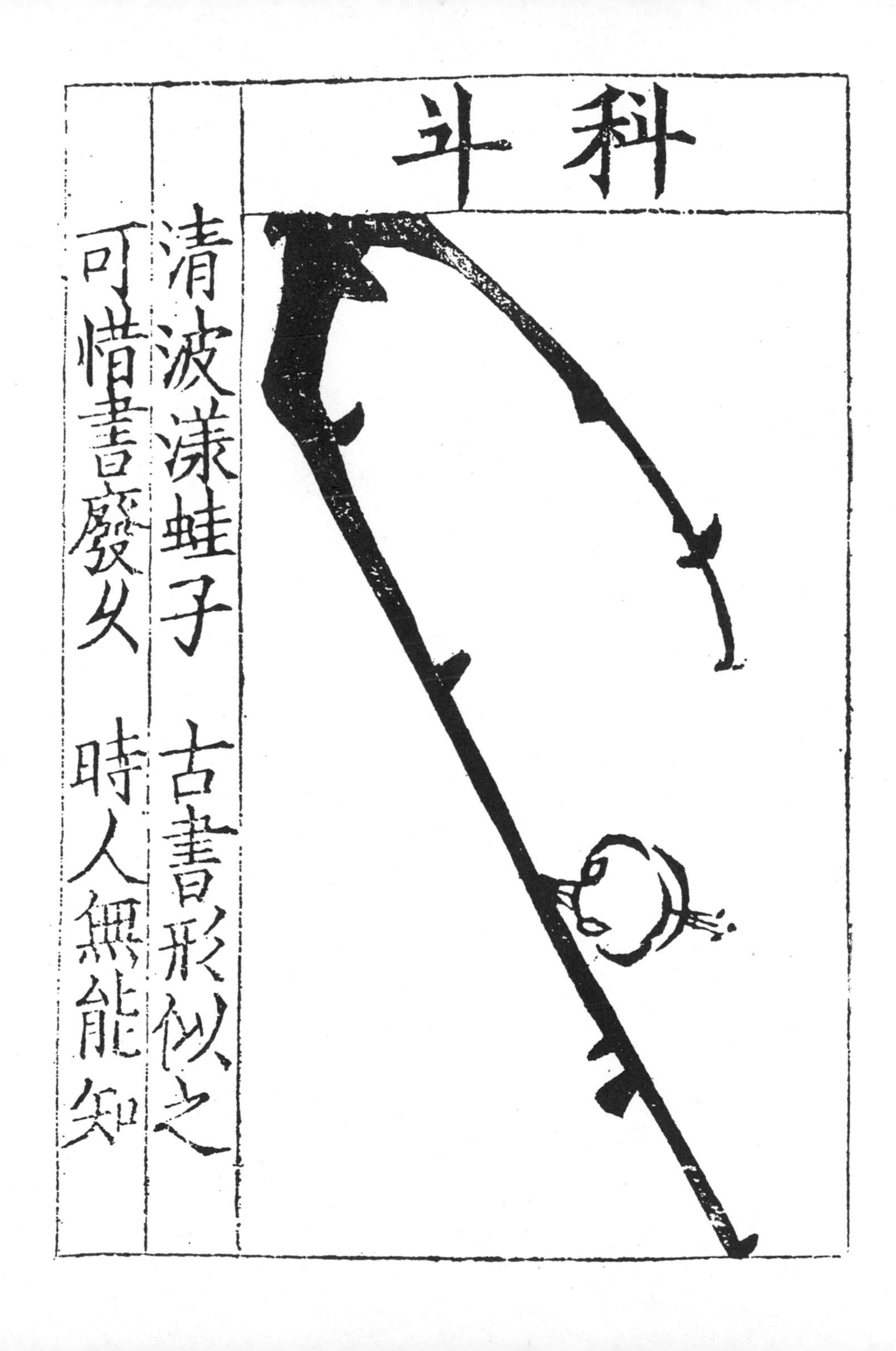
科斗
清波漾蛙子 古書形似之
可惜書廢久 時人無能知

Big Petals

Eight Branches

21 *Zither Pick*

high-mountain sounds or flowing water
crystal notes from a fingertip
play them not for common people
lest you rouse Po Ya's wrath

The Chinese trace the seven-string zither back 5,000 years to Emperor Fu Hsi, who is also credited with inventing the trigrams of the *I ching* or *Book of Changes*. The instrument is traditionally played with bamboo picks attached to the forefinger and thumb. Po Ya played his zither some 3,000 years ago from a hill overlooking the confluence of the Han River and the Yangtze. Whenever he played, his friend Chung Tzu-ch'i knew what was in his heart. Sometimes it was high mountains. Sometimes it was flowing water. When Chung Tzu-ch'i died, Po Ya smashed his zither, claiming there was no one else worth playing for. Po Ya's "High Mountains" and "Flowing Water" are still in the repertoire of Chinese zither players.

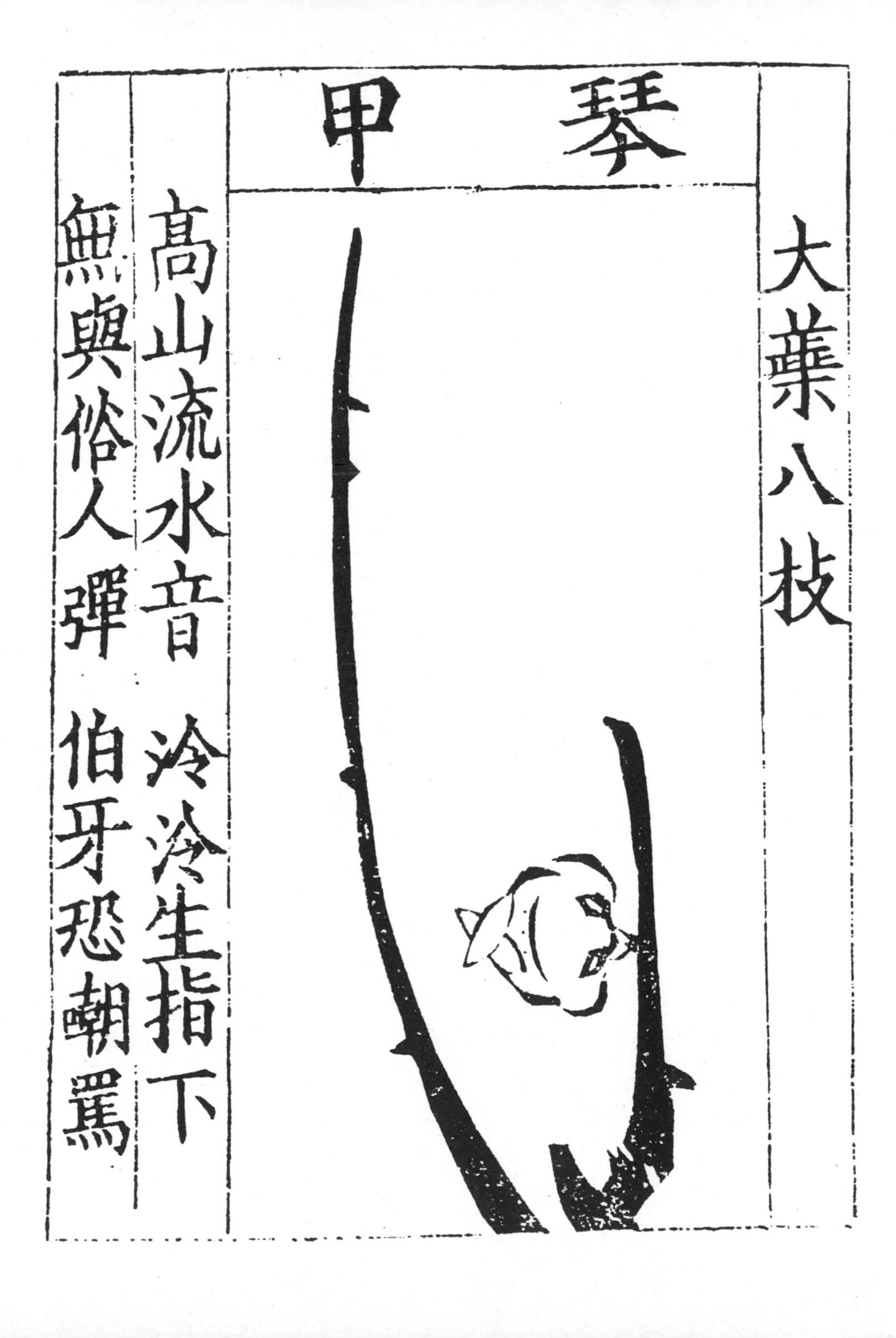

琴甲
大葉八枝
高山流水音 泠泠生指下
無與俗人彈 伯牙恐嘲罵

22 *Pestle*

inside Toad Palace there's a hare
grinding elixir for millions of years
elixir that gives eternal life
beyond the reach of mortals

Toad Palace is another name for the moon and the residence of Heng-o (also known as Ch'ang-o), the wife of Hou-yi. Long ago, one of the daughters of the Queen Mother of the West gave Hou-yi a pill that conferred immortality. But she warned him that dire consequences would result if he swallowed it before he was physically and spiritually ready. Hou-yi returned home and hid the pill. Then one day, when he was gone, his wife discovered the pill and swallowed it. It made her so light, she floated up to the moon, where she turned into a toad and coughed up the pill, which turned into a hare. And the hare has been busy ever since grinding more elixir for Heng-o.

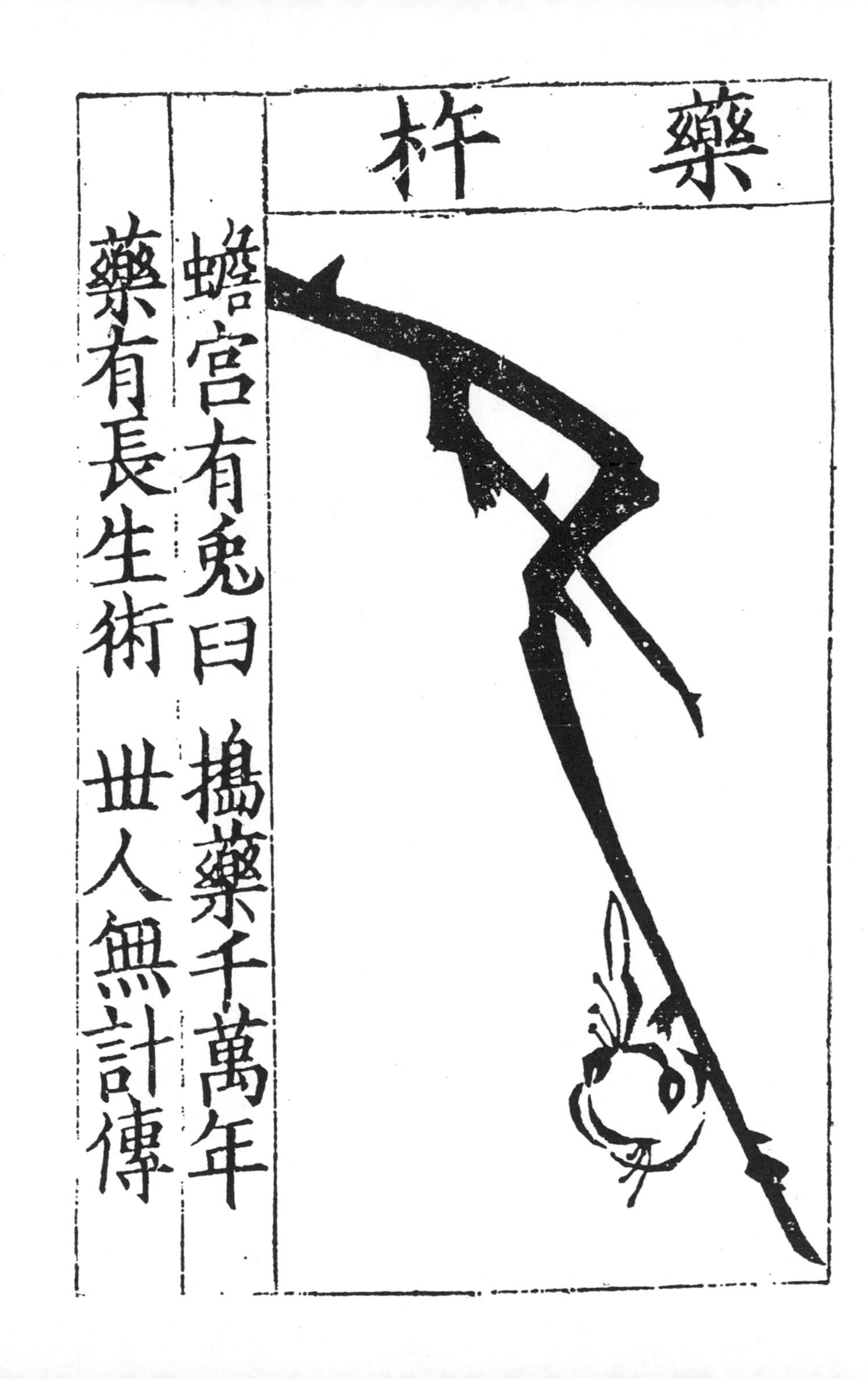

藥杵
蟾宮有兔曰 擣藥千萬年
藥有長生術 世人無計傳

23 *Oyster Shell*

don't quarrel with a snipe
there's a line between land and water
neither should you harbor pearls
they won't guard your life

The state of Chao once attacked the state of Yen, and the king of Yen proposed launching a counterattack. The king's advisor objected and related the following story: An oyster was sunning itself on a riverbank, when suddenly a snipe flew down and speared it. But before the snipe could eat the oyster, the oyster slammed shut on the snipe's beak, and neither creature would let go of the other. Eventually, a fisherman came along and ate them both for dinner. The advisor said that attacking Chao would only expose Yen to the attack of a third state, which is, in fact, what happened in the third century B.C., when both Yen and Chao were swallowed by the state of Ch'in.

蚌殼

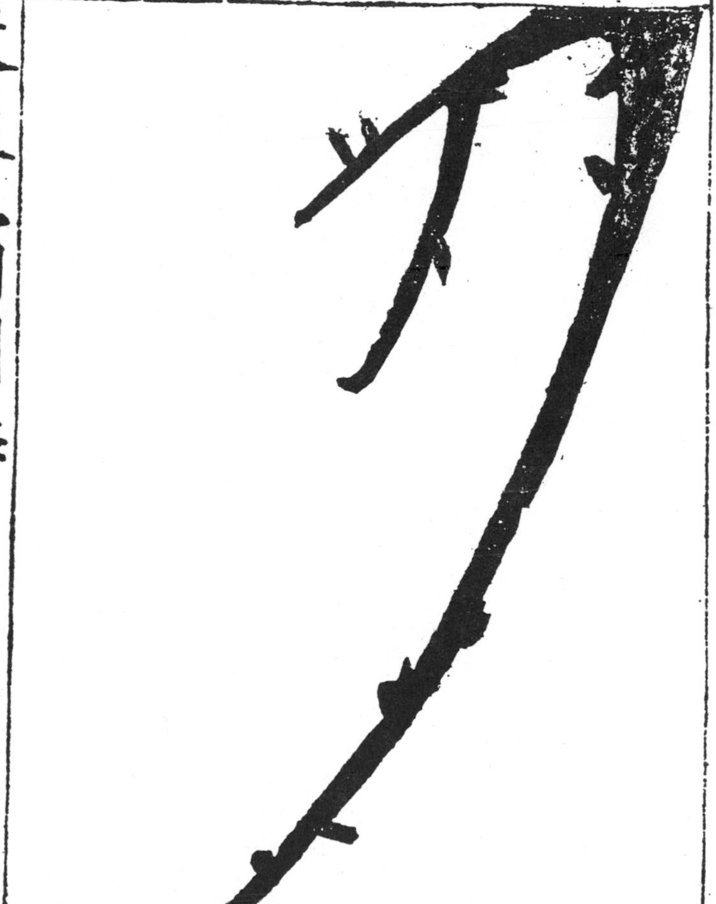

伏與鷸相持　自有山川隔

祝君無孕珠　恐非保身策

24 *Stork Beak*

atop a pine it strains and sings
no different from a Yangchou crane
though a crane it never will be
doomed to wear this black disguise

The crane is a symbol of purity and transcendence, and on its back Taoists fly to the Islands of the Immortals—if, indeed, they don't become cranes themselves. Once, at a dinner party, a host asked three guests to reveal their secret fantasies. One said he imagined himself becoming governor of Yangchou. Another said he imagined himself becoming a fabulously wealthy merchant. The third guest said he imagined himself flying off on a crane. The first guest then combined the fantasies of all three and said he imagined himself wrapping 10,000 strings of coins around his waist and traveling to Yangchou on the back of a crane. Ever since then, the Yangchou crane has been a symbol of greed rather than transcendence. The stork's appearance is similar to the crane's, except for its black beak.

鶴觜

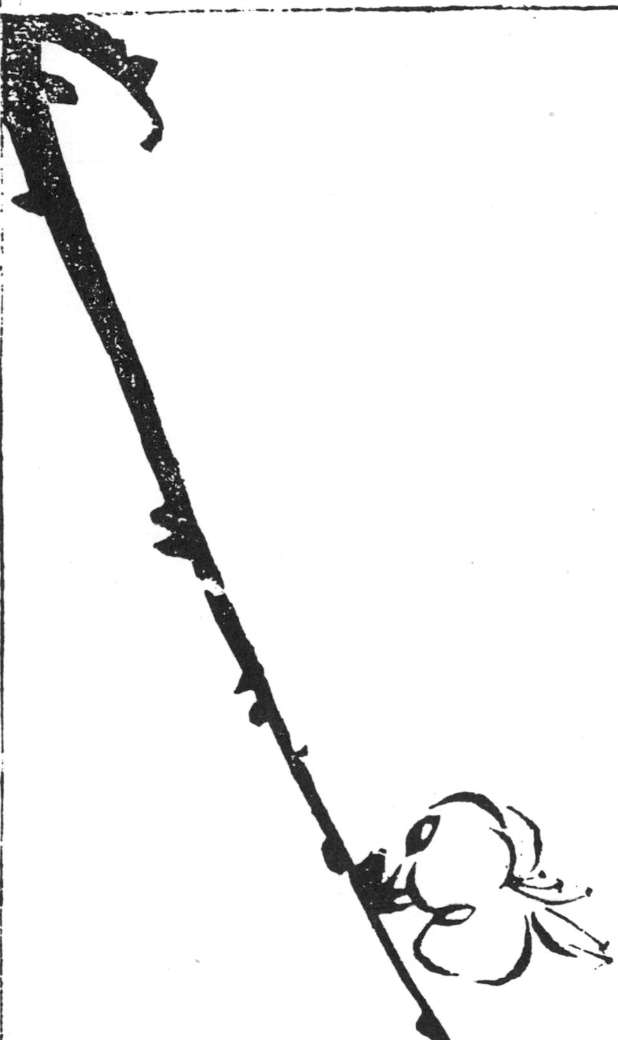

曳頸吟松梢 何異揚州鶴
胡爲鶴未成 苦被玄裳錯

25 *Yu*

a larger vessel dignifies the sacrifice
it's filled before the *ch'ang* is served
and used in turn to fill the *yi*
rituals have their order

In ancient times, the shaman and other participants at a sacrifice were served an alcoholic beverage called *ch'ang*, which was distilled from black millet and infused with turmeric. The ch'ang was first poured into a large bronze vessel called a *yu* and carried into the ceremony by means of a bronze handle attached to either side of the vessel that allowed it to swivel and thus avoid spillage. The ch'ang was then ladled into smaller bronze vessels called *yi*, from which the participants drank.

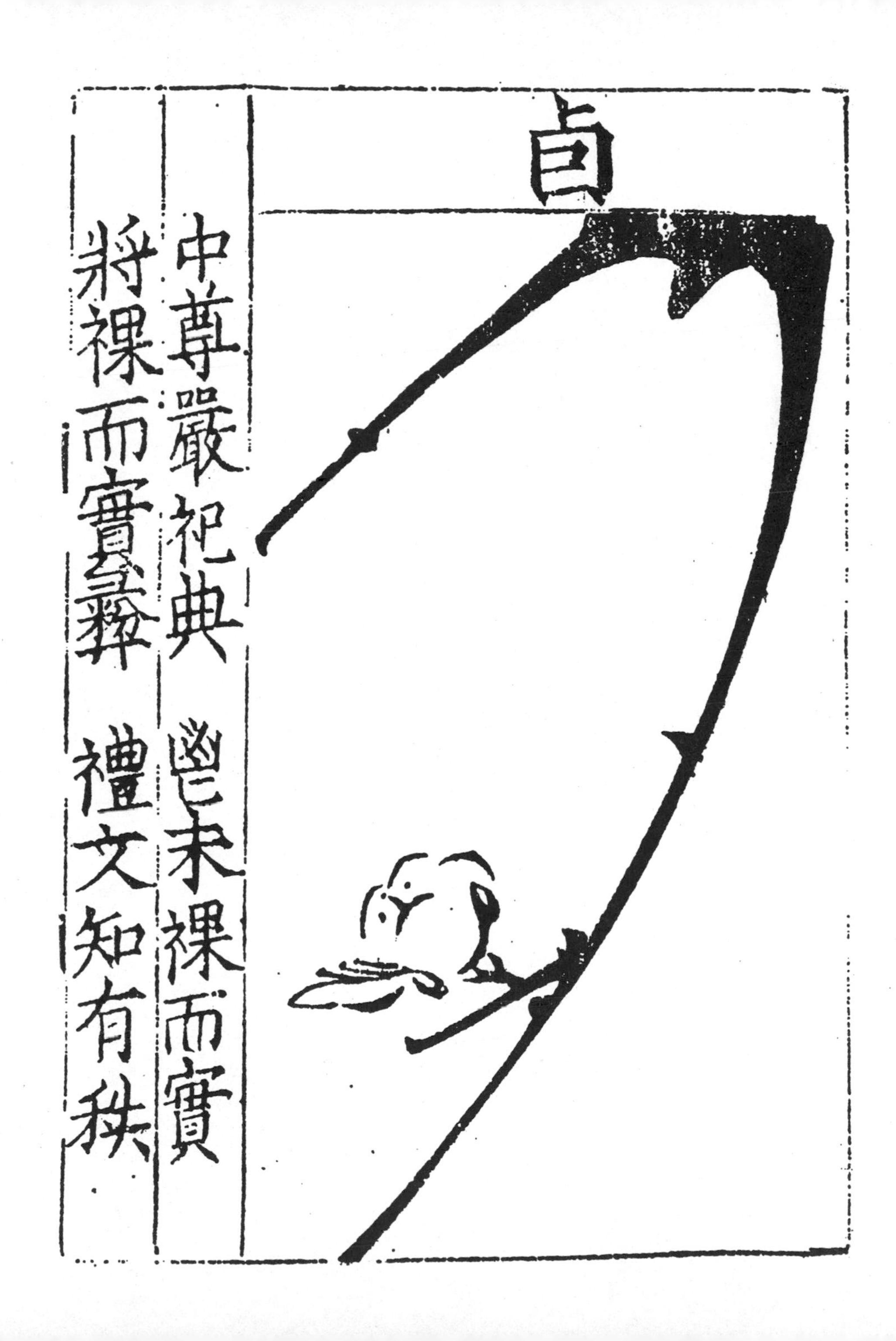
卣
中尊嚴祀典
豈未祼而實
將祼而實彝
禮文知有秩

26 *Chu*

sides and depth of fixed dimensions
struck it sets the tune
to stop the music tap the *yu*
start and finish have their cues

The *chu* and *yu* were among the percussion instruments of the early Chinese and are now rarely used, except on such ritual occasions as Confucius' birthday (September 28). The chu was a square wooden box twenty-nine inches on a side, twenty-one inches deep and open at the top. It was struck on the inside at the beginning of a performance to establish the beat for an ensemble. The yu was a hollow wooden instrument carved into the shape of a tiger. Its back was tapped to announce the end of a performance.

柷

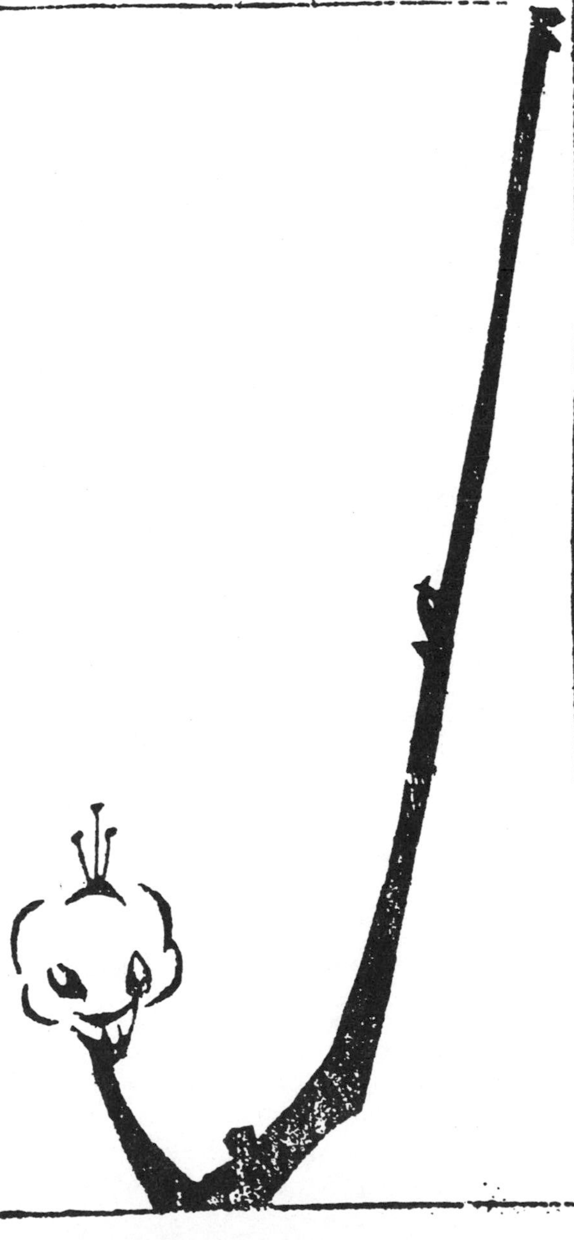

方深有制度　撞之以合樂
止樂戛以敔　始終知所覺

27 *Pien*

green bamboo with weft of white
shaped not unlike a *tou*
during the sacrifice what does it hold
dried peaches meat and grain

The *pien* consisted of a pedestal woven of rattan or bamboo and an upper bowl that held four pints of offerings. Offerings that included sauces were placed inside a similar vessel made of pottery—and later bronze—called a *tou*. Tou of clay dating back 6,000 years have been found among the earliest neolithic remains in China. Because of their association with longevity, peaches are a favorite offering to gods, ancestors, and elders.

籩

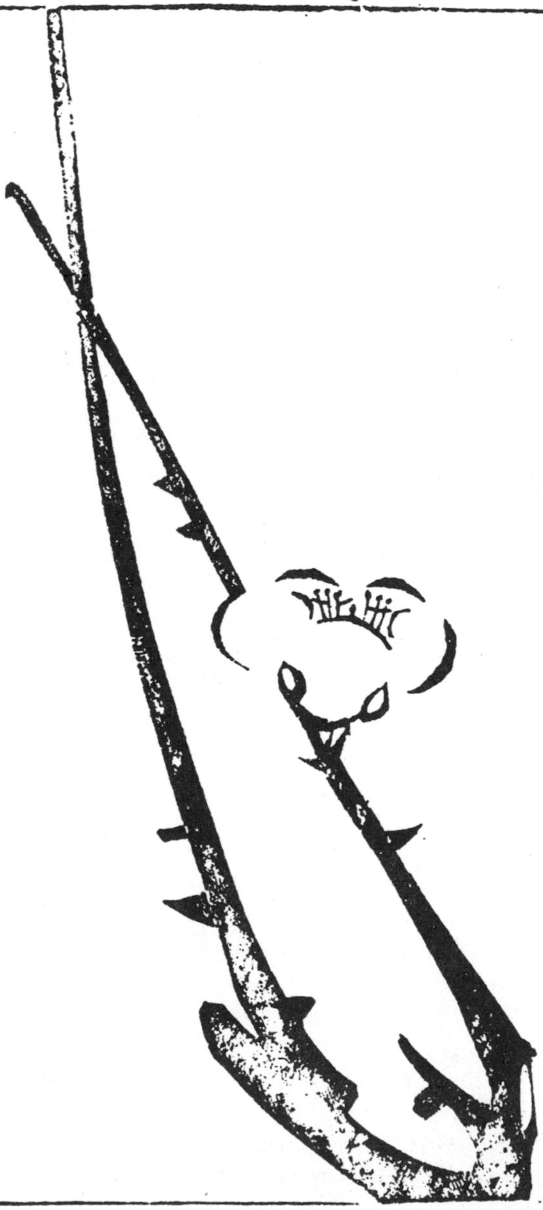

蒼竹緯琅玕　爲形有如豆
遇祭何所容　乾桃與脩糗

28 *Chueh*

posts make sure it isn't drained
it only holds a pint
knife-like legs give warning
a gentleman takes care

The *chueh* was a small bronze vessel supported by three bladed feet. It was used to hold the *ch'ang* mentioned in number 25 and was originally called an *yi*. It was renamed by Sung dynasty scholars because it reminded them of a small bird ("ch'ueh:sparrow") whose call sounded like "stop-stop, enough-enough." They also thought the two posts that protruded from the top of the chueh were meant to come into contact with the drinker's forehead if he tried to drain the vessel and to remind him when to stop. This may have been true for certain chueh, but most of the vessels unearthed so far have rudimentary posts. And the earliest ones, dating back 4,000 years, have no posts at all.

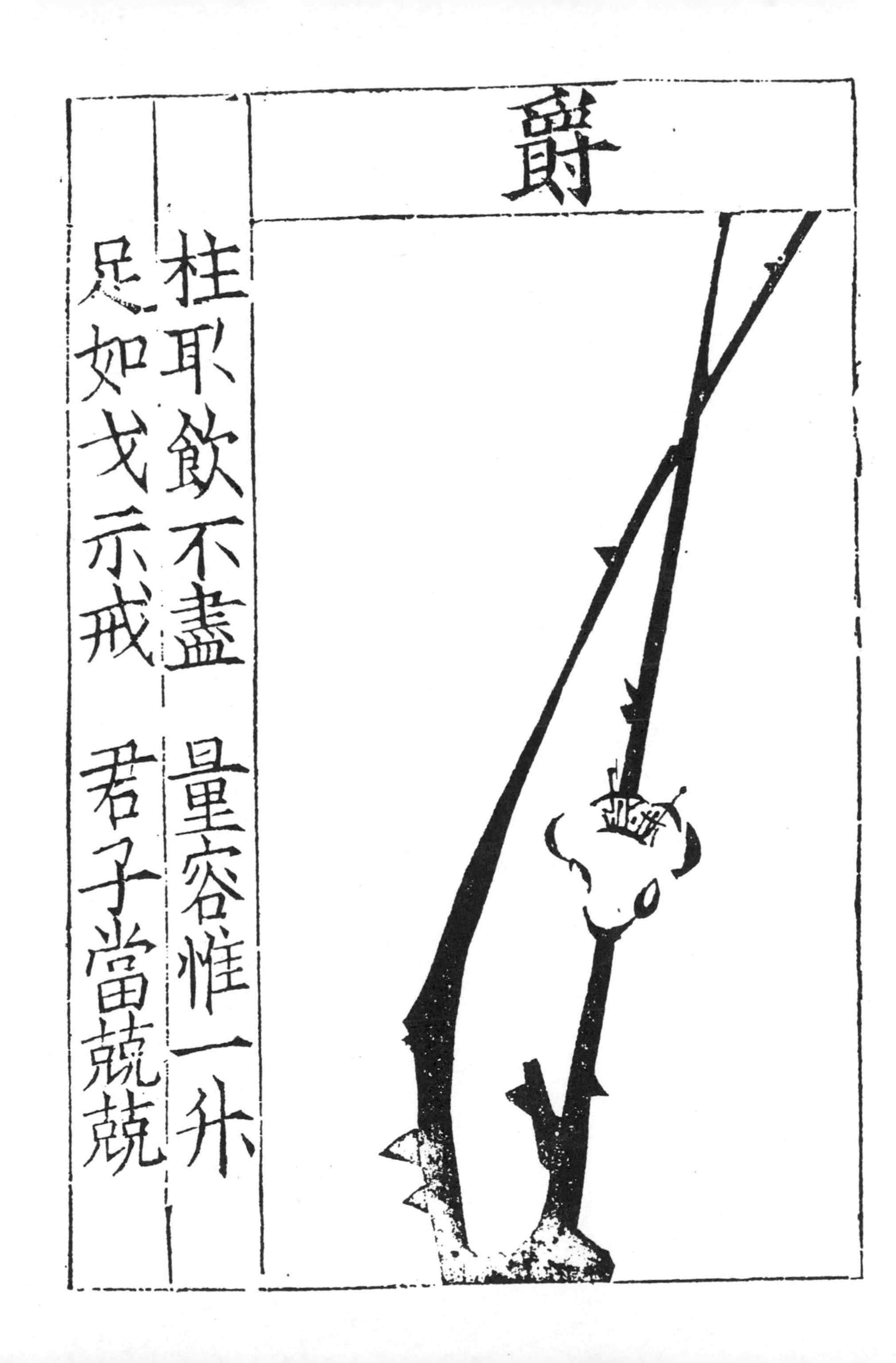
爵
柱耳欲不盡 量容惟一升
忌如戈示戒 君子當兢兢

Opening

Eight Branches

29 *Jug of Spring Perfume*

drunk on a quart drunk on a gallon
the only limit is no disorder
no one knows if you alone are sober
on a riverbank distraught and forlorn

Spring wine is made during the winter from rice or other grain harvested the previous fall. The hill tribes of southwest China still carry on this tradition, as I can personally attest, which supplies the means to drive away the winter and to welcome the spring. Since the alcoholic content of rice wine is rarely more than 10 percent, someone who gets drunk on a quart is considered to have a low tolerance. The eighth-century poet Li Pai, however, is said to have been capable of writing a hundred poems while drinking a single quart.

The second line is from the *Analects* of Confucius, of whom it was said, "It was only regarding wine that he set no limit. As long as he wasn't disorderly." (Ch. 10) But this is easily misconstrued. This was the Sage's attitude regarding proper behavior during a sacrifice. Elsewhere, Confucius advises his disciples not to be overcome by wine. (Ch. 9) The last two lines are culled from the beginning of Ch'u Yuan's poem "The Fisherman": "When Ch'u Yuan was banished / he wandered along rivers / he sang on their banks / distraught and forlorn / till a fisherman asked / aren't you the Lord of the Gorges / what fate has brought you to this / and Ch'u Yuan answered / the world is muddy / I alone am clean / everyone is drunk / I alone am sober / and so they sent me away."

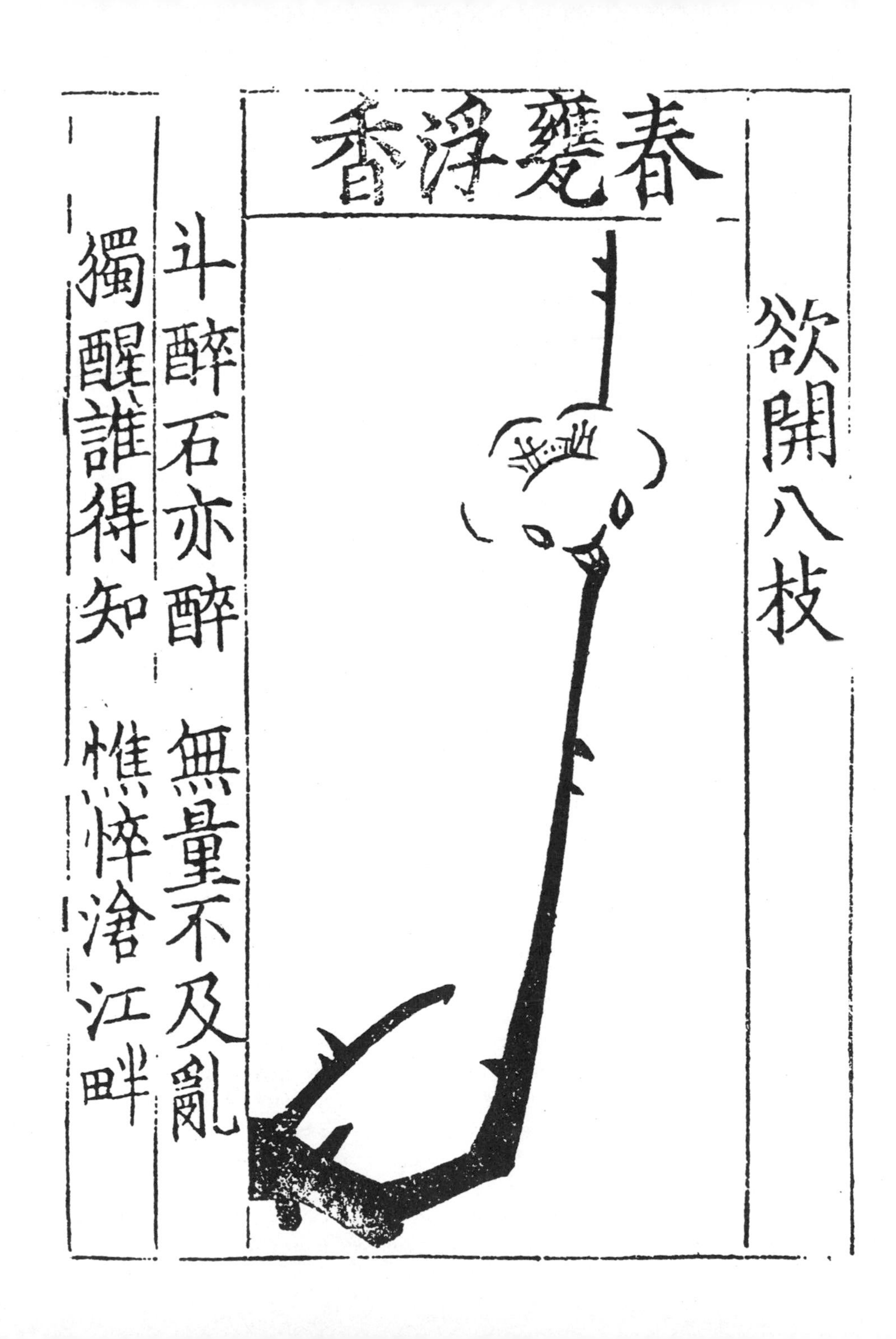

春甕浮香
欲開八枝
斗醉石亦醉
無量不及亂
獨醒誰得知
憔悴滄江畔

30 *Cold Pot Flame*

lamplight chases autumn chill
single-minded men see glory
ten hard years beneath a window
favored by a golden lotus

The Chinese still carry bowls or pots of charcoal, often suspended on wires, to warm themselves in winter. The title suggests an old scholar still trying to pass the exams that lead to official appointment. The first line, from a poem by Sung dynasty poet Chu Sung, introduces us to a candidate of modest means studying at night beneath a neighbor's window and dreaming of arriving as Ling-hu T'ao once did at the Hanlin Academy, where the emperor's senior officials lived. After passing the exams, Ling-hu rose to the post of chief minister under T'ang dynasty Emperor Hsiuan-tsung, and he served in that capacity for ten long years. One night after working late in the palace, the emperor bestowed on him the singular honor of being carried back to the Hanlin Academy in the imperial carriage, which was lit in front by gilded candles shaped like lotuses. Ling-hu T'ao's fellow officials were most impressed.

寒釭吐焰

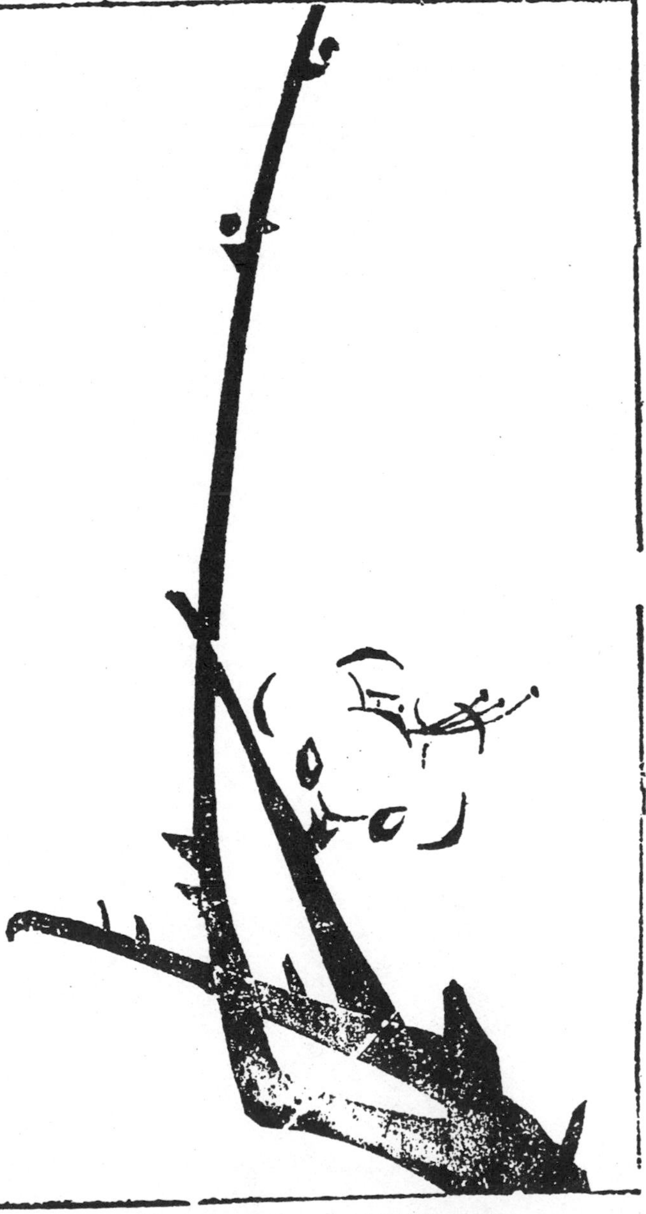

燈火迫新涼　志士功名重

十年窗下愁　會見金蓮寵

31 *Snail Horns*

which is stronger Man or Ch'u
locked in endless warfare
fighting over empty names
using up the people's strength

Chuang-tzu once used the example of a snail to urge people to shun the counsel of war. The horns of a snail, he said, were two countries named Man and Ch'u that were engaged in an endless cycle of warfare over the empty space that stretched between them (*Chuangtzu,* 25).

蝸角

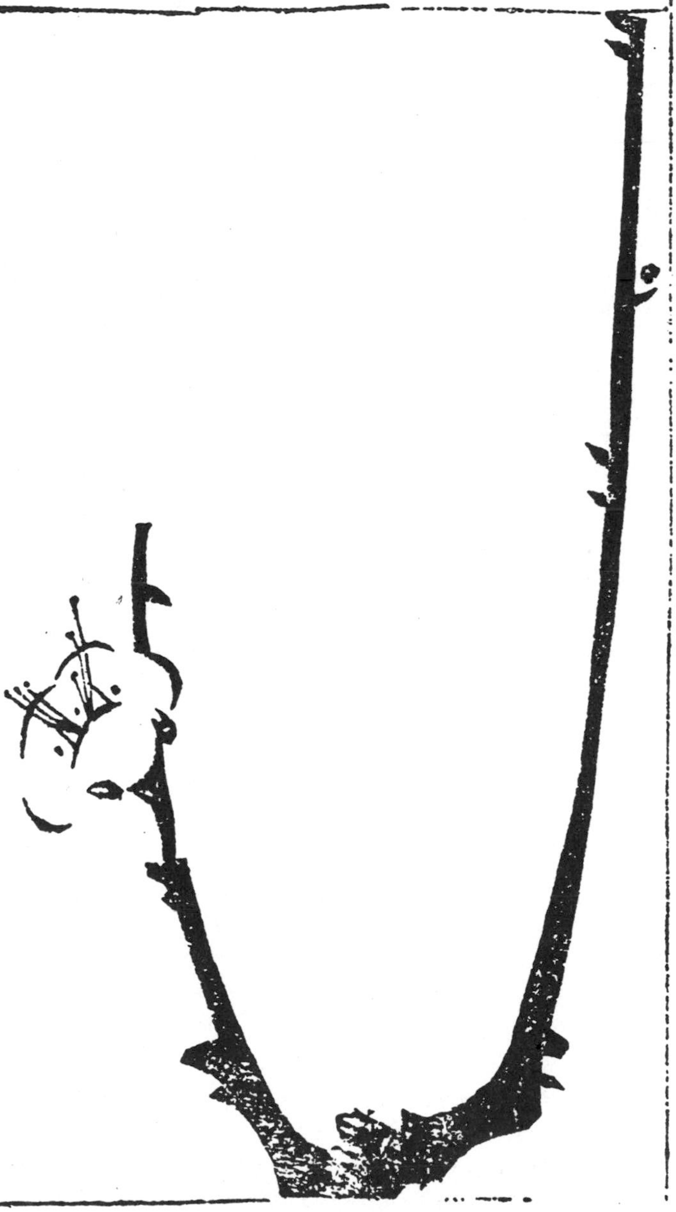

蠻觸國誰雄　戰爭猶未息

由此奪虛名　費盡人間力

32 *Horse Ears*

what's Ch'i-chi without Po Le
thin pointed useless knives
on North Terrace deep in snow
read the poem of old Tung-p'o

Po Le lived around 900 B.C. and was a famous judge of horses. In his treatise on the subject, he listed the characteristics of a horse's ears as indicative of its ability. Their size and sharpness, he said, revealed a horse's stamina and speed. Among the horses whose ears justified his theory was Ch'i-chi, whose name is still synonymous with speed. Scholars seeking official positions have often expressed the hope of finding a ruler as perceptive as Po Le. Su Tung-p'o once wrote two poems on the wall of Chucheng's North Terrace after a heavy snowfall. In one of them, he wrote that the only things visible above the snow were the twin peaks of Horse Ear Mountain.

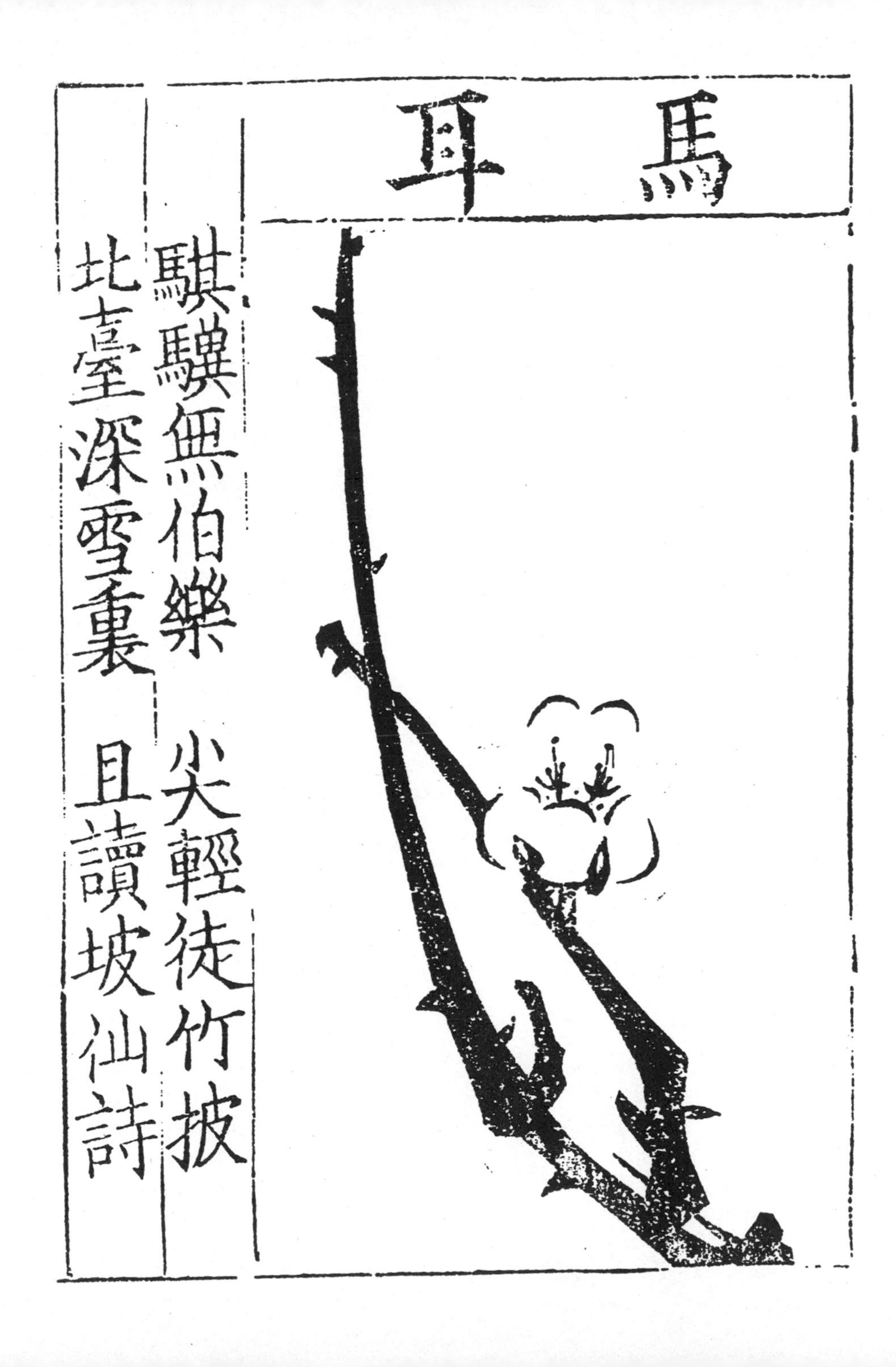
馬耳
騏驥無伯樂
尖輕徒竹披
北臺深雪裏
且讀坡仙詩

33 *Kuei*

the ancients prized ritual vessels
this one held the millet
inside square outside round
no doubt a special container

The *kuei* was a wooden vessel used for holding millet during sacrifices. It stood one foot high and had a capacity of one peck and two pints. Its counterpart for holding rice was the *fu,* which had the same capacity but was square on the outside and round on the inside. Rice was the chief grain of the south, while millet was the chief grain of the north. Both vessels were fitted with a lid, on top of which sat a turtle. The turtle symbolized the universe, and in the case of the kuei the square interior symbolized Earth, and the round lid symbolized Heaven.

簋

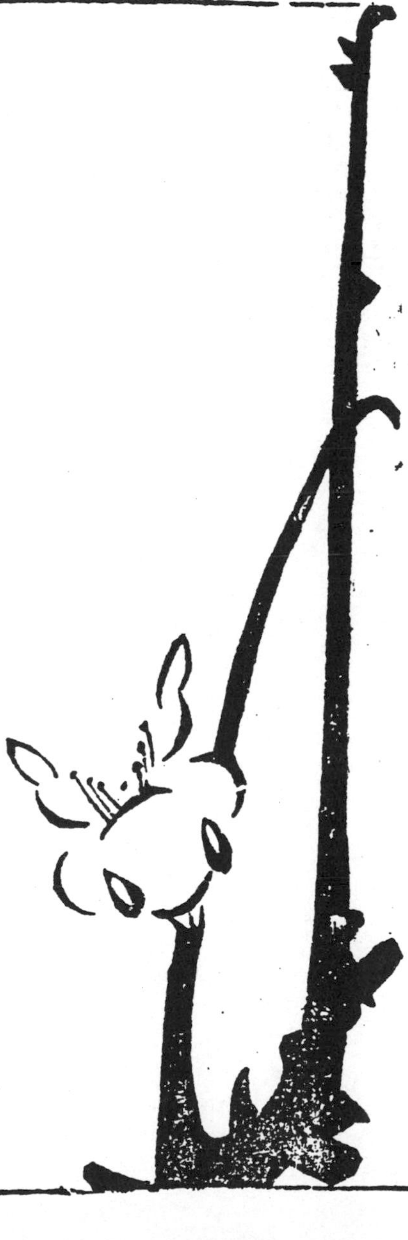

祭器古不輕　斯焉盛黍稷

內方而外圓　無乃器之特

34 *Tsan*

imagine a bowl with a handle of jade
a ladle for pouring libations
serving the *ch'ang* one cup at a time
who could forget its ancient meaning

The *tsan* was used during ancestral sacrifices to serve the *ch'ang*, as explained in number 25. This particular ritual utensil consisted of a jade handle attached to a bowl ten inches in diameter with a capacity of five pints. The character "tsan" is made up of two parts: one meaning "jade," the other meaning "assist" or "offer up."

瓚

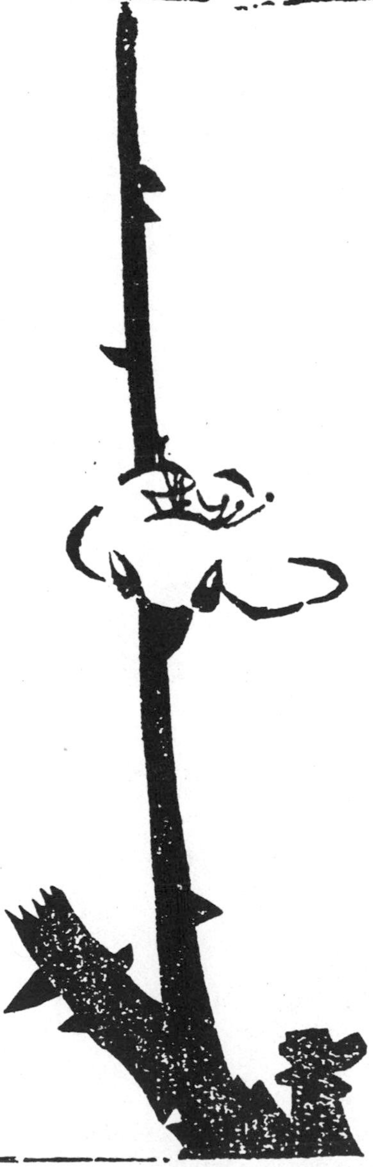

如盤而柄圭　崇裸以爲器

秬鬯次第陳　豈容忘古意

35 *Gold Chop*

Su Ch'in whipped his horse harder
he lived on the wind of six states
authority dangled at his elbow
alas no country retreat

Signatures still have no legal status in China. Only when a vermilion seal has been affixed with a chop made of metal, stone, bone, or wood is a document recognized as genuine. In ancient times, a person's chop was attached to his waist sash to prevent its misuse. Only a prime minister or his representative was allowed to use a gold chop. Su Ch'in, who lived in the fourth century B.C., was an architect of the coalition of six states that opposed the encroachment of the state of Ch'in. The great authority that he wielded, however, depended on his constant travel among the different states, and he was rarely able to visit his home in Loyang. He was murdered while living as a guest in the state of Ch'i, unlike his teacher, the Taoist Kuei Ku, who slipped quietly away and lived out his days in anonymity. To spend one's final years in the countryside was the dream of most officials in ancient China.

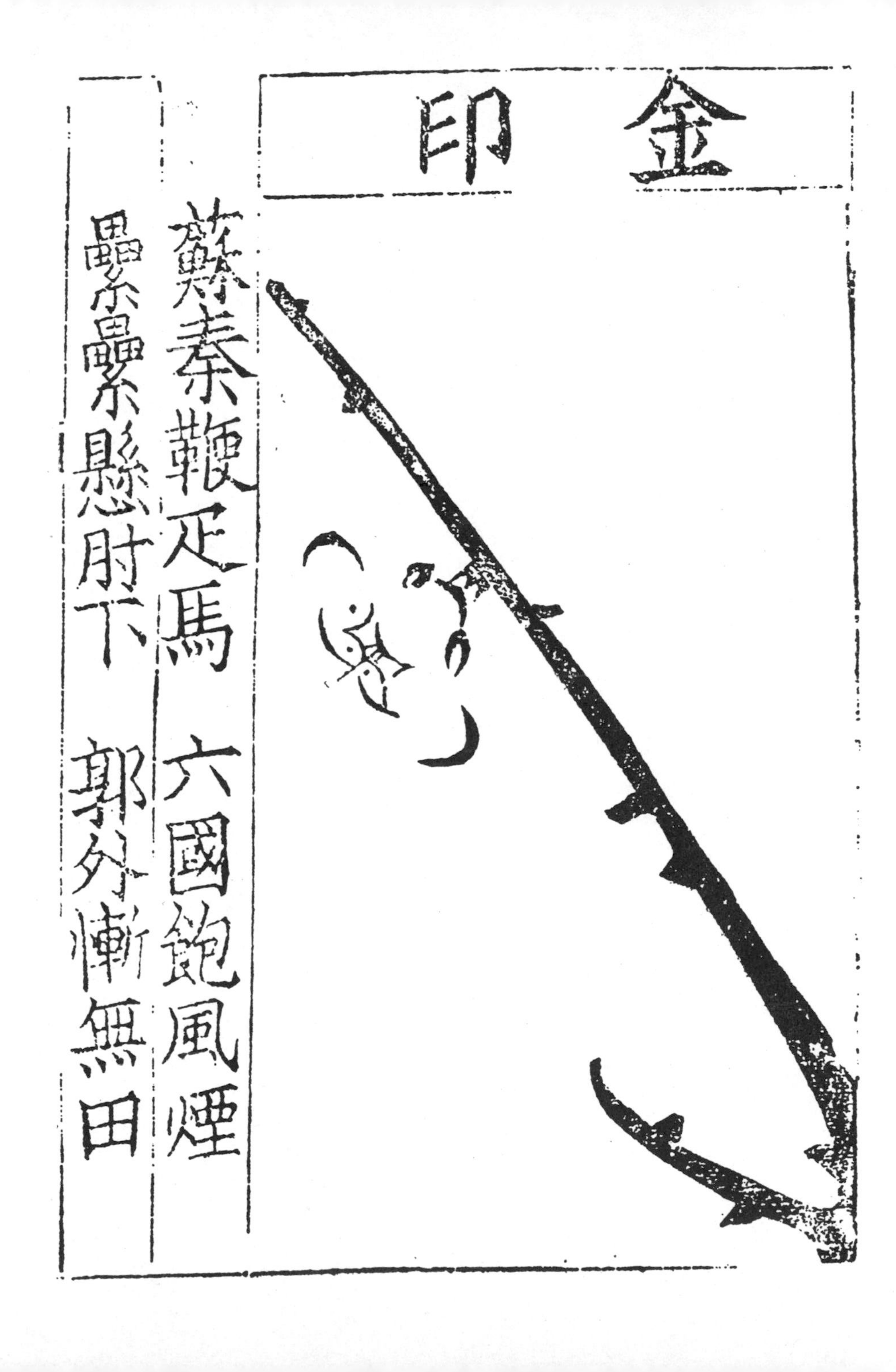
金印
蘇秦鞭疋馬
六國飽風煙
纍纍懸肘下
郭外慚無田

36 *Jade Dipper*

at Hungmen the drinking stopped
the sword dance didn't work
Fan Tseng struck in vain
the Han belonged to Liu

Hungmen is the name of an opening in the loess plateau east of the ancient capital of Ch'ang-an. This is where Hsiang Yu and Liu Pang met in 206 B.C. to divide the empire after bringing the Ch'in dynasty to an end. At their meeting, Hsiang Yu planned to assassinate his rival during a sword dance, but Liu Pang's advisor learned of the plot and convinced Liu to act the fool. Hsiang Yu forgot to give the signal, and Liu escaped during a visit to the latrine. Before he left, Liu asked his advisor to present two jade dippers to Fan Tseng, Hsiang Yu's chief advisor who had hatched the assassination plot. Realizing their chance to stop Liu had slipped away, Fan Tseng smashed the dippers in anger. Not long afterward, Liu Pang defeated Hsiang Yu and established the Han dynasty.

玉斗

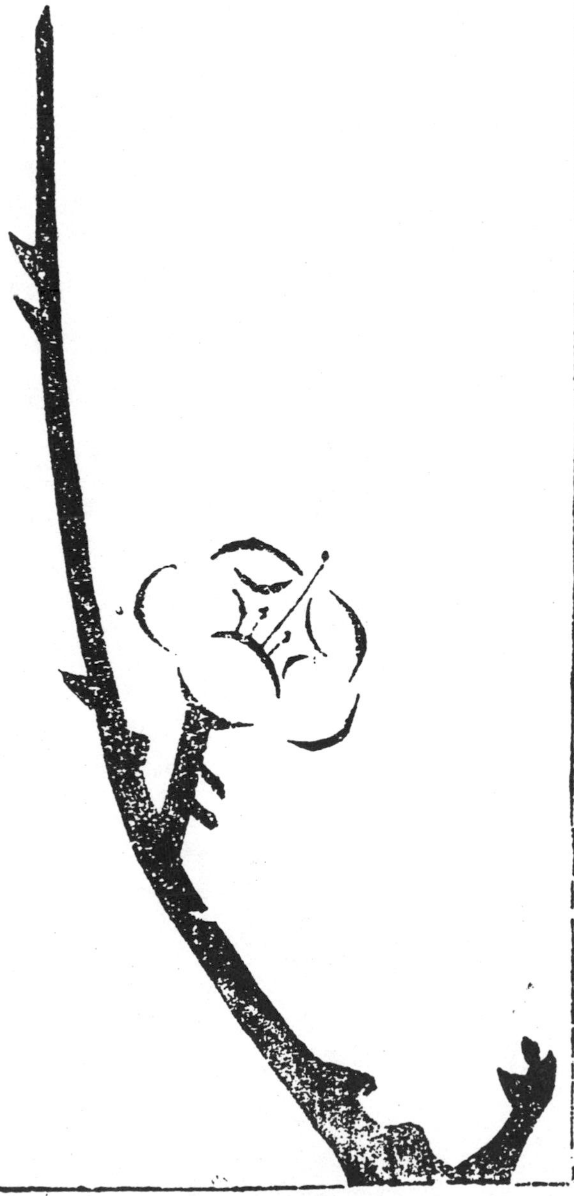

鴻門罷樽酒　舞劍事還差

范增徒怒撞　漢業成劉家

Fully Opened

Fourteen Branches

37 *Yi*

colored silk on formal robes
indicates instruction follows
tigers and monkeys on temple bronzes
stand for filial piety

Yi was the general term for a bronze vessel used as a cup or a vase during sacrifices in the ancestral temple. Such vessels, cast with monkey or tiger designs, have been traced back some 4,000 years to the time of Emperor Shun. Shun was chosen to succeed Emperor Yao because of his filial piety, and the tigers and monkeys were intended to remind people that even the most vicious and unruly of beasts honored their parents. Shun is also credited with adding to court attire silk robes embroidered with twelve symbols that included the monkey and the tiger.

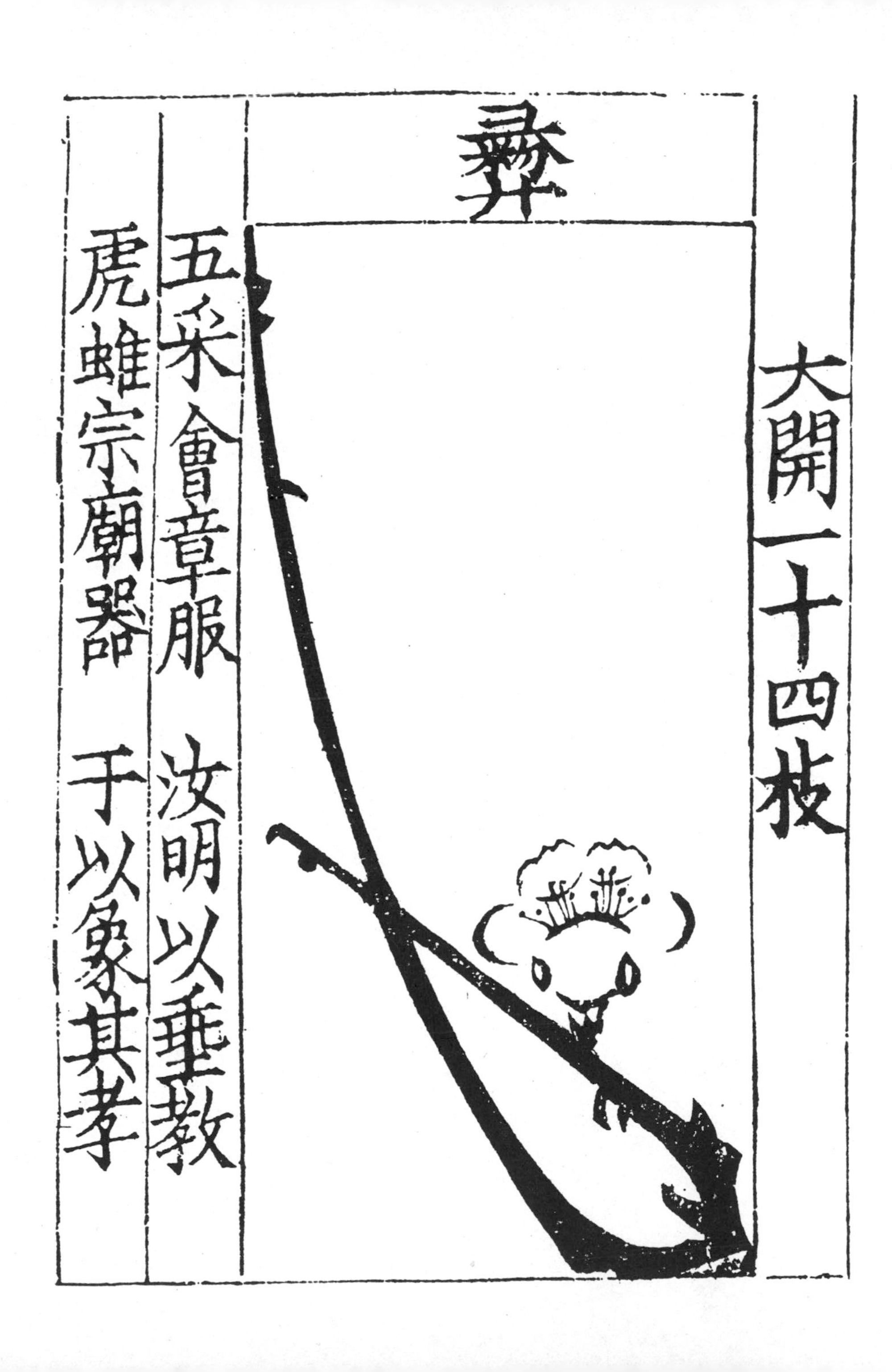
彝
大開一十四枝
五采會章服　汝明以垂教
虎蜼宗廟器　于以象其孝

38 *Fu*

symbols take twelve forms
the ax shape is no toy
double-edged it means distinguish
here it means decide

As mentioned in the previous note, silk robes worn at court were embroidered with twelve symbols that were already ancient when Emperor Shun began using them more than 4,000 years ago. In addition to the tiger and the monkey, they included two axes. The double-edged version symbolized the ability to distinguish right from wrong, while the single-edged version, or *fu,* depicted here, symbolized the power to decide.

黼

象明十二章　斧形不可玩

黻以取其辨　斯以取其斷

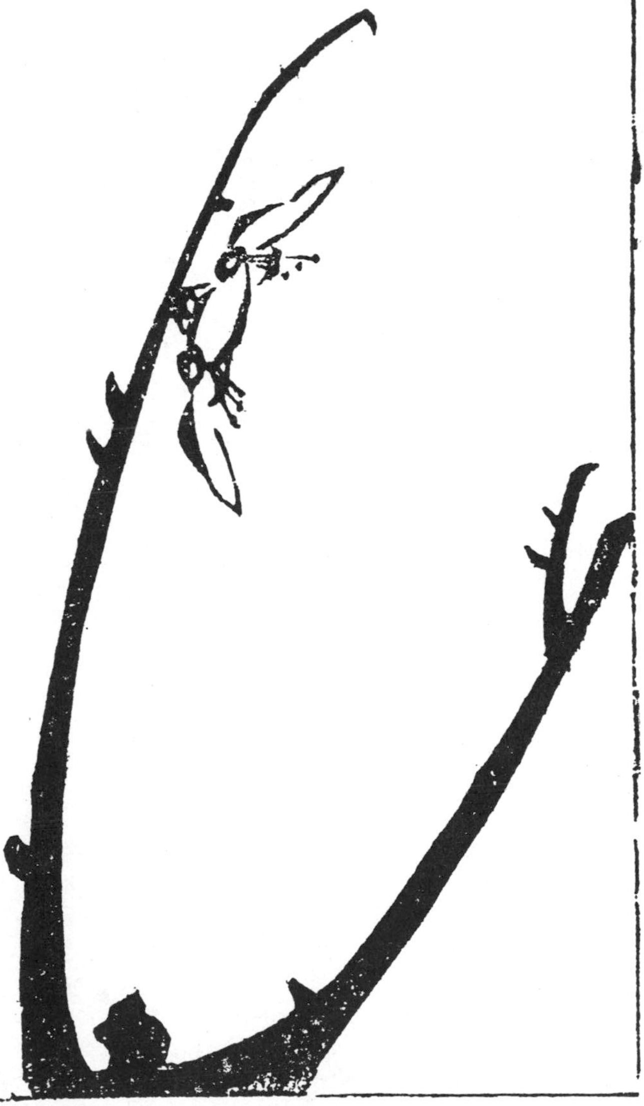

39 *Tilting Bowl*

fill it and it empties
more or less are both mistakes
all things have a balance
don't think this one isn't right

This "bowl-on-a-swivel" was placed next to the throne to remind the emperor that whatever was full would soon be empty. Only when the bowl was half-full was it stable. According to Hsun-tzu, Confucius saw a device like this in the ancestral hall of Duke Huan: "An attendant poured water into a container that hung at an angle. As the water level approached the midpoint, the container became upright. But when the attendant went beyond the midpoint, it tipped over, the water poured out, and only after it was empty did it resume its former position. Seeing this, Confucius sighed, 'Alas! Whatever becomes full becomes empty!'"

欹器

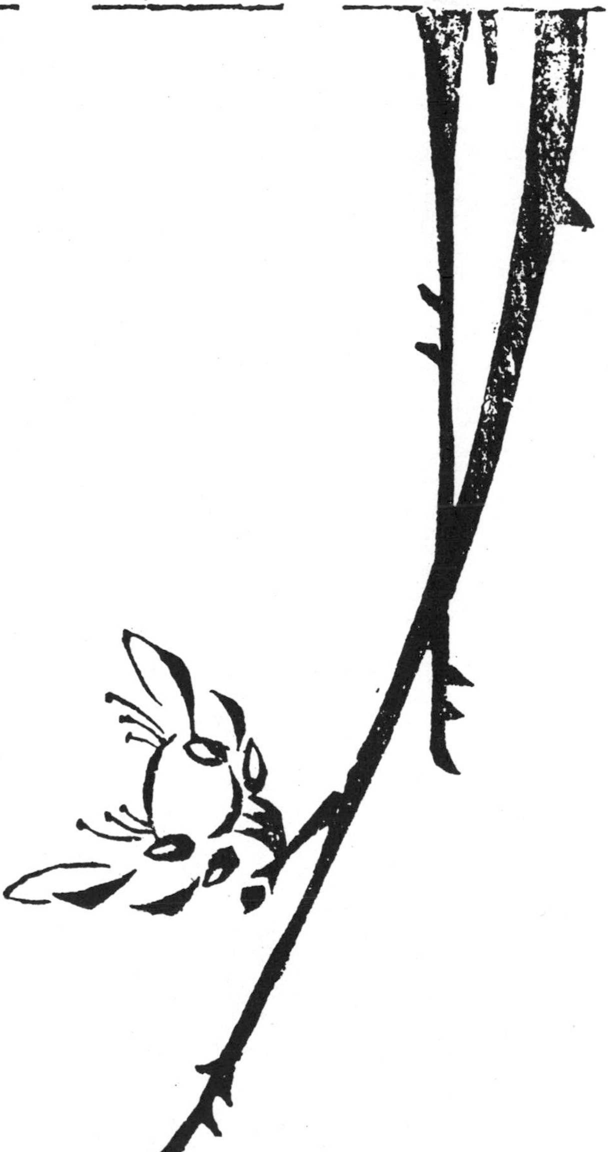

溢滿而覆虛　盈虧俱有病

萬事得于中　烏乎云不正

40 *Hanging Bell*

from the hills it sings of dawn
the sinking Dipper the waning moon
it calls out to greedy people
the treadmill never ends

This type of bell can be found in Buddhist or Taoist temples, where it still announces services before dawn. Although every city had its quota of temples, most were built beyond city walls so that their residents might have an easier time freeing themselves of delusion, hate, and greed —the poisons that perpetuate rebirth on the Wheel of Life and Death.

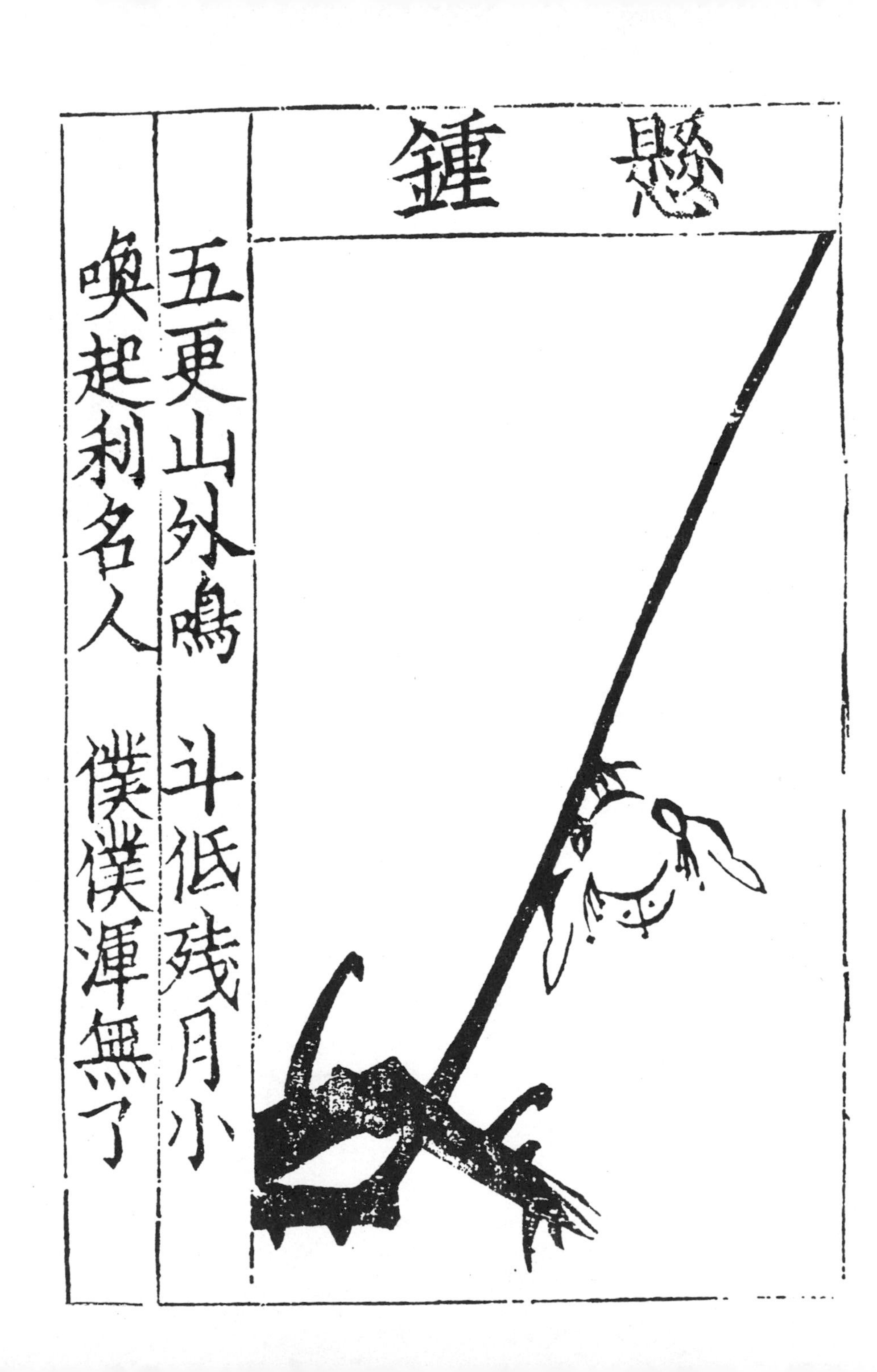
懸鍾
五更山外鳴　斗低殘月小
喚起利名人　僕僕渾無了

41 *Fan*

Nine Flowers and Six Corners
hand down different names
rather may you soothe the people
stir for us a gentle breeze

In the third century A.D., the emperor gave a fan described as having nine flowers on it to Ts'ao Ts'ao, who later removed him from the throne and brought the Han dynasty to an end. A century later, a man offered to inscribe the hexagonal fans that an old lady was selling along a promenade. To her surprise, she sold the fans for a small fortune. The man turned out to be Wang Hsi-chih, China's most famous calligrapher. Thus the name Nine Flowers is associated with misfortune and the name Six Corners with good fortune. Also in the fourth century, the famous writer-official Yuan Hung, on being presented with a fan to cool himself with while on a journey to his new post, replied, "Rather may it stir a gentle breeze to soothe the people."

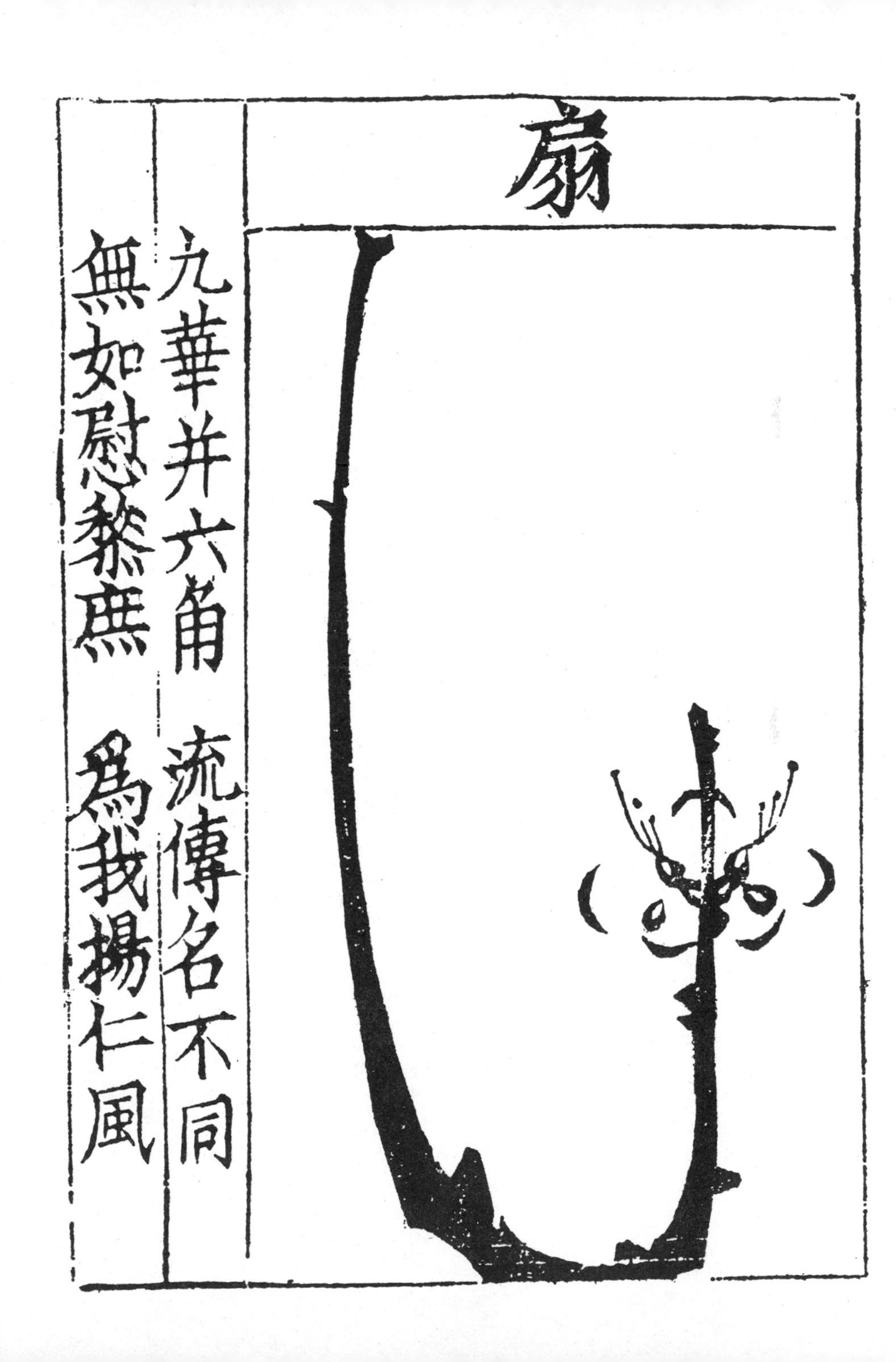
扇
九華并六角　流傳名不同
無如慰黎庶　為我揚仁風

42 *Basin*

swimming silver fins in crystal
glassy luminescence
engraved with *ever new*
the ages bow to T'ang of Shang

Bronze basins were used for washing the face and hands during rituals, and their inner surface was often cast with turtles, fish, and other creatures of the deep. On the washbasin of Emperor T'ang were inscribed the words: "May you renew yourself today, renew yourself day after day, renew yourself every day." T'ang overthrew the Hsia dynasty in 1750 B.C. and founded the Shang dynasty, which he named after the small fiefdom where he began his rebellion. T'ang's quest for self-renewal continues to inspire the Chinese, as it did Sun Yat-sen, the founder of modern China, who changed his name during his early years to Jih-hsin ("Ever-new").

盤

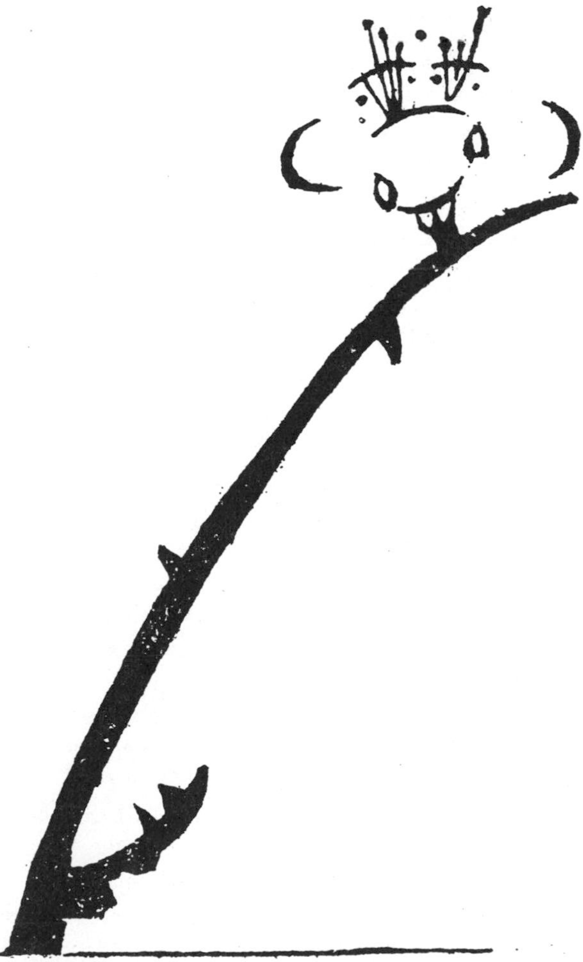

水精行素鱗　琉璃走夜光

銘垂日日新　萬古稽商湯

43 *Facing the Sun*

looking toward Ch'ang-an
men of will await a mission
peas and sunflowers have one thought
how can Heaven turn away

Located beneath the streets of modern Sian, Ch'ang-an was the biggest city in the ancient world, with more than 2 million residents. It was the capital of eleven dynasties and the center of the Chinese universe from the time it was first built in 200 B.C. until it was destroyed in A.D. 907. Four centuries later, in Sung Po-jen's day, Ch'ang-an remained a watchword for the Golden Age of Chinese culture. Sung's fellow expatriates south of the Yangtze dreamed of driving the barbarians from north China and reuniting the country, with Ch'ang-an as its capital. Peas and sunflowers are heliotropic, and members of China's official class often referred to themselves as such, always looking toward the Son of Heaven. Here, Sung bemoans the royal reluctance to take up the challenge of reunification.

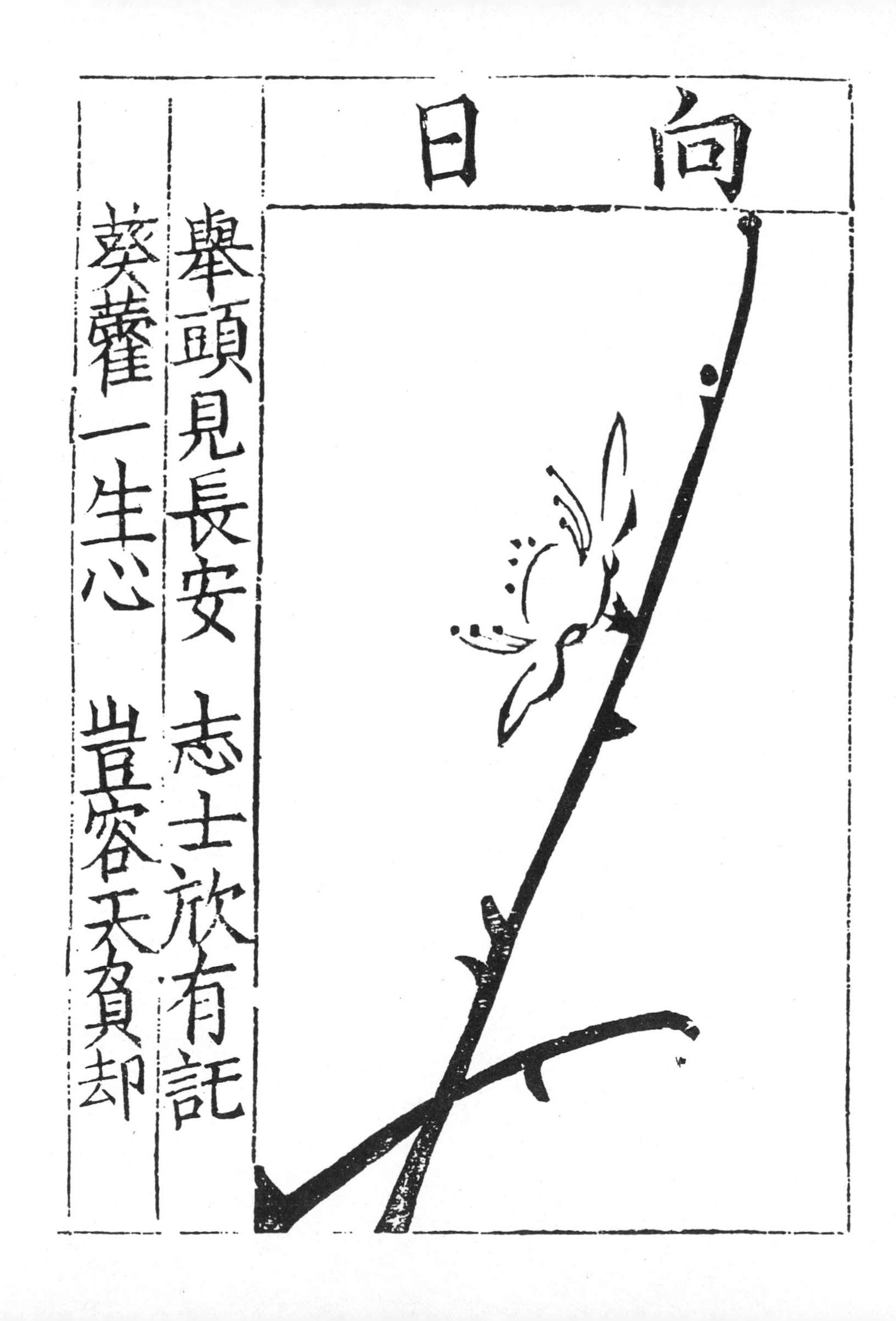
向日
擧頭見長安 志士欣有託
葵藿一生心 豈容天負却

44 *Collecting the Dew*

where now lies the Immortal's Hand
a thousand years of useless shame
chrysanthemums in the ancient garden
drenched with dew on Double Ninth

The drinking of dew, the purer the better, was considered efficacious in prolonging life. To this end, in the second century B.C., Emperor Wu constructed a tower of cedar beams and bronze pillars more than 200 feet high. And on top of this tower he placed a bronze basin to collect the dew of the gods. The basin became known as the Immortal's Hand and was probably buried with Emperor Wu at Maoling, some forty kilometers west of Sian. This wasn't the only extravagance indulged in by Emperor Wu in his search for immortality, and Sung Po-jen voices the Confucian disdain for such waste of public funds on personal fantasies. The Chinese words for "chrysanthemum," "old," and "nine" are all homophones. And on the ninth day of the ninth month (nine being the ultimate *yang* number, and the combination of two nines being especially auspicious), elderly Chinese still celebrate their longevity with infusions of chrysanthemums.

擎露

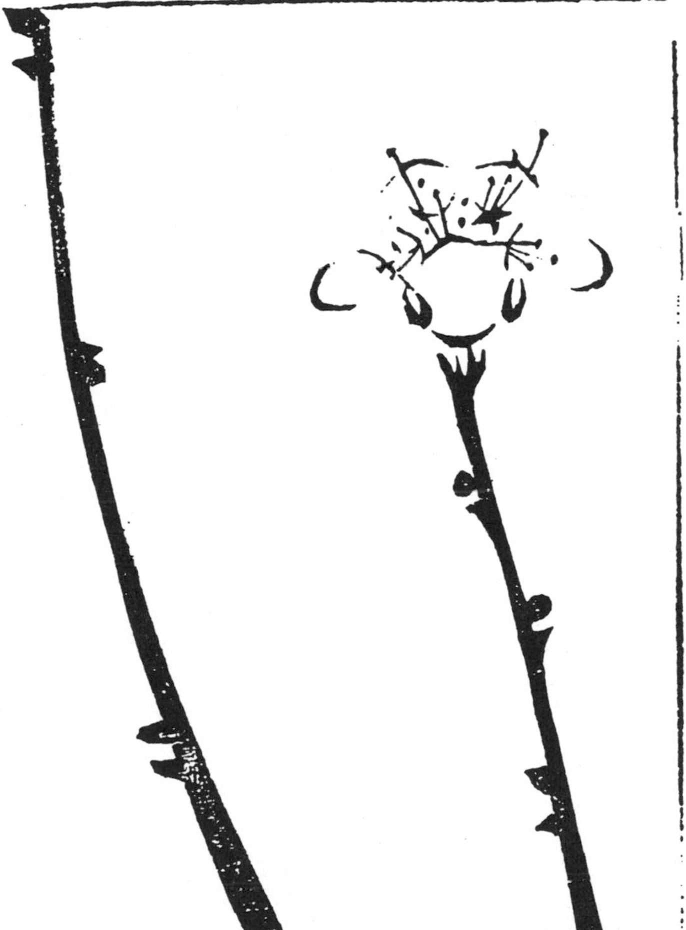

僊掌在何處　徒成千載羞
唯有故園菊　沾濡當九秋

45 *Tripod*

from Chiaju to Fenyin
their fame still free of rust
people hunger for a chef
someone who can cook

The tripod, with its three legs supporting a round or square body, first appeared in neolithic times as a clay cooking pot that was heated from underneath. In addition to its use in cooking the family dinner, it was also used for presenting offerings to ancestors. As the second function began to take precedence over the first, tripods were made of bronze at great expense, and the possession of such a vessel conferred the right to conduct sacrifices to clan ancestors.

Around 1000 B.C., King Ch'eng of the Chou dynasty set up a tripod at Chiaju, just west of Loyang, to establish his clan's authority over the Yellow River and the Huai River floodplains. Fenyin is the name of a place in Shansi province where a tripod was unearthed in the second century B.C. that reportedly belonged to the Yellow Emperor, who reigned around 2600 B.C. Confucius and his followers considered the period between the Yellow Emperor's reign and the Chou dynasty as China's age of sage rulers. Lao-tzu says, "Ruling a great state is like cooking a small fish," (Ch. 60) and the *Book of Documents* says, "In making soup, be my salt and plums." (4.8)

鼎

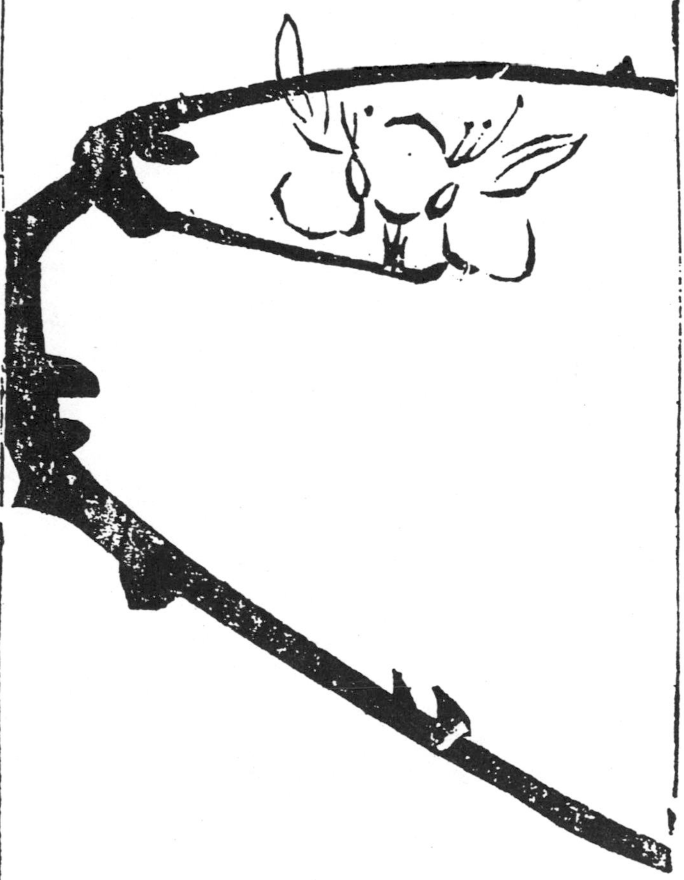

郟鄏至汾陰　重名垂不朽
天下望調羹　有誰能着手

46 *Bell*

among the palace rattle drums
hangs an empty-bellied bell
Confucius heard it once in Ch'i
for ninety days he ate no meat

In 517 B.C. Confucius left his own state of Lu during a period of political instability and took up residence in Lintzu, the capital of the neighboring state of Ch'i. While he was there, he heard a style of music first developed by the music master of Emperor Shun 1,700 years earlier. The music was called *Shao,* and Confucius was so overwhelmed by it that he didn't pay attention to food for three months. Although primarily orchestrated for wind instruments, it also included drums and bells. This particular kind of bell doesn't have a clapper but is suspended from a wooden frame and struck from the outside. It is now used primarily in Confucian temples. Hand-held rattle drums are struck by balls suspended on either side of the barrel.

鏞

堂下雜簴鼗　如鍾而聲腹

夫子聞於齊　三月不知肉

47 *Antlers*

the does all bleat
the woods and mist say fall
the moon above Kusu Tower
where Wu Tzu-hsu once strolled

Sung Po-jen must have had in mind this couplet from "Spirit Tower" in the *Book of Songs*: "The king is in his spirit park / the does so sleek and tame." Kusu, or Lingyenshan as it's now called, is the name of a hill fifteen kilometers southwest of Suchou in Kiangsu province. During the fifth century B.C., King Fu Ch'ai of the state of Wu turned the hill into a deer park. After defeating the state of Yueh to the south, he built a palace and a huge tower on the hill and spent much of his time banqueting here with his new concubine, Hsi Shih, a gift from the state of Yueh. His chief minister, Wu Tzu-hsu, criticized him for his dalliance and later paid for his frank advice with his life. Wu Tzu-hsu is much revered by the people of Suchou, as it was he who chose this site for Wu's new capital.

麋角

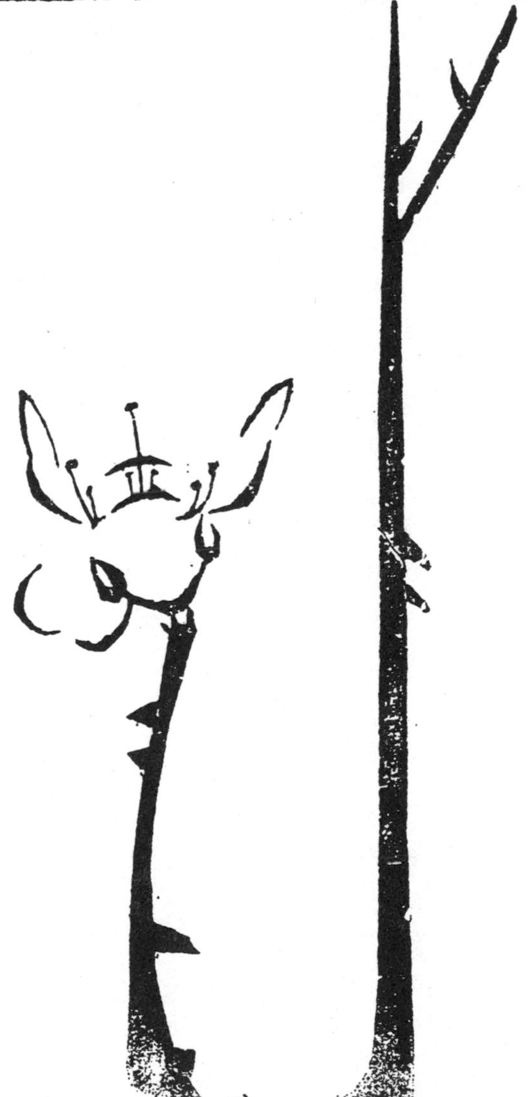

麀鹿同呦呦　山林風雨秋
姑蘇臺上月　子胥曾約遊

48 *Gibbon Arm*

where she hears a howl
the moon is cold and gates are few
she asks each crane she meets
when will my lord return

According to the *Paoputzu,* a Chinese army entered the mountains of southern China around 1000 B.C. and was never seen again. The officers turned into gibbons and cranes, and the soldiers became insects and sand. Gibbons were once common in the mountains of the south, and travelers reported hearing their eerie howls the entire length of the Yangtze Gorges. The arm bone of the gibbon was once used to make flutes. The only gibbons left in the wild in China are restricted to several nature reserves in the extreme south. Cranes also refer to Taoist recluses.

猿臂

一聲長嘯處　霜月淒林扉
與鶴每相問　貴人胡未歸

49 *Pinched Eyebrows*

why must others imitate
Hsi Shih's ceaseless frown
better just to giggle
it won't ruin your rouge

Hsi Shih was one of the most famous beauties of ancient China. In the fifth century B.C., the king of Yueh presented her to his nemesis, the king of Wu, to distract him from attending to government affairs—an assignment in which she succeeded. Among her famous attributes were pinched eyebrows, reportedly caused by a heart condition. When other women heard how beautiful she was, they tried to copy her frown but only succeeded in making themselves look foolish.

顰眉

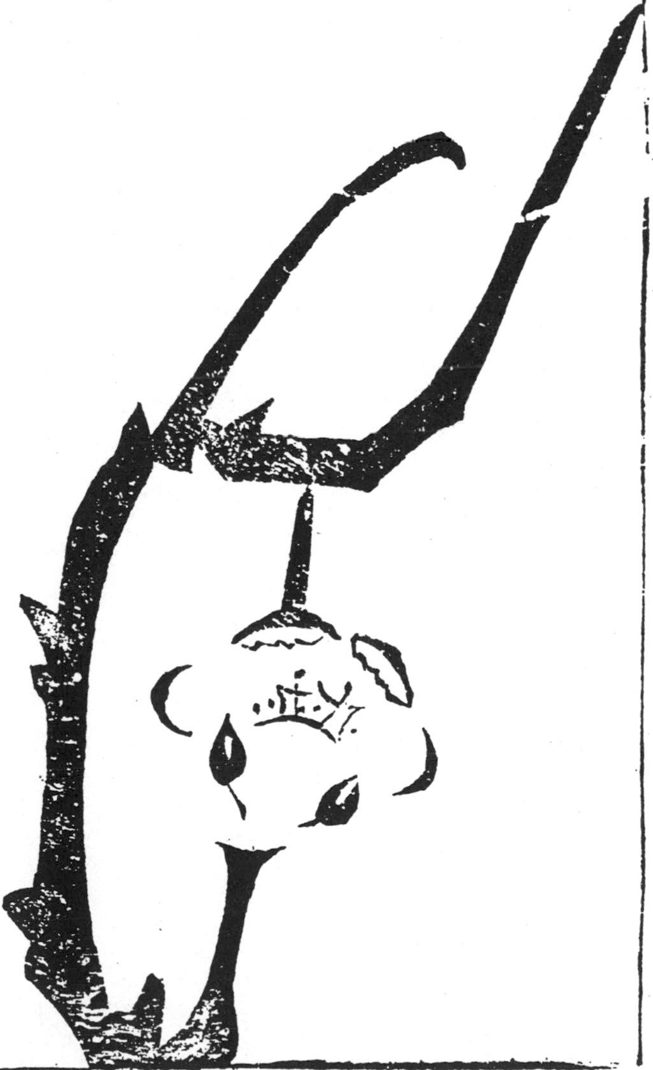

西施無限愁　後人何必傚
只好笑呵呵　不損紅粧貌

50 *Profile*

face to face is problematic
watching from the side is better
otherwise neither knows
the other's nostril length

An old Chinese adage advises, "From the side the view is clear / from in front no one sees." The Chinese practice of physiognomy assigns great importance to the length of a person's nostrils, with longer nostrils indicating greater depth of character.

側面

相見是非多　但虧觀覷了

庶無人共知　鼻孔

梅花喜神譜卷上終

Radiant

Twenty-eight Branches

51 *Lifting the Mirror*

opening the *ling*-flower case
revealing the lovely and ugly
frightening how many heroes
the sudden attack of white hair

Bronze mirrors entered China along the Silk Road as early as 4,000 years ago. They remained the primary means of reflection until the eighteenth century, when they were finally replaced by glass. These early mirrors were rarely bigger than a person's hand but were sufficiently convex to reflect the whole face. The back was covered with symbols and designs and included a protruding boss in the middle with a cord that allowed the mirror to be picked up from its protective box without getting fingerprints on the polished side. Most mirrors were round, although a popular shape during the T'ang and Sung dynasties was the eight-petalled *ling* flower, a variety of water chestnut. It reminded those who used it of the purity of water and of water's ability to reflect their true appearance.

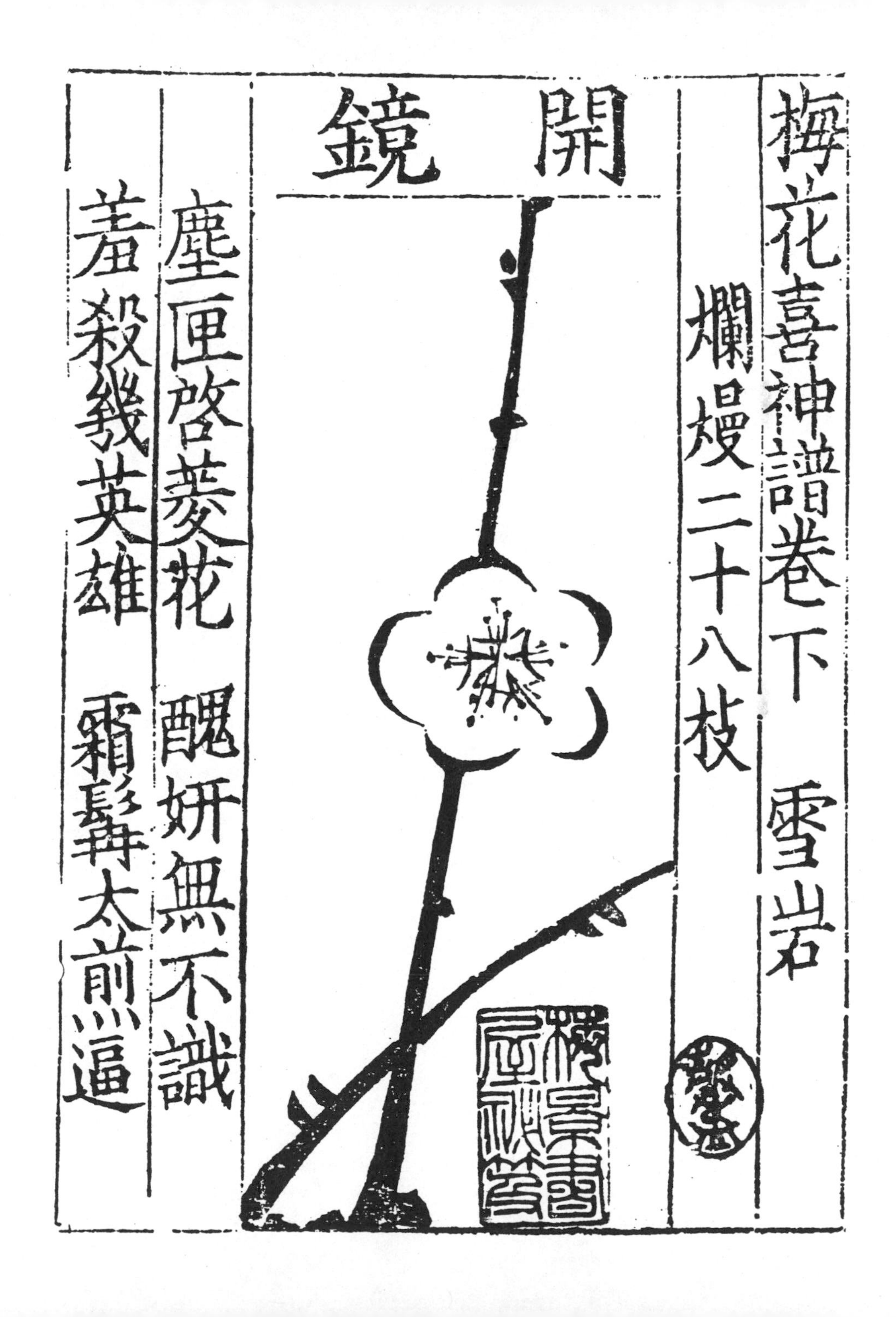

梅花喜神譜卷下　雪岩

爛熳二十八枝

開鏡

塵匣啓菱花　醜妍無不識
羞殺幾英雄　霜鬚太煎逼

52 *Overturned Cup*

who sighs the moon is lovely
breaking through the winter sky
a drunk who's never sober
no need to pour more wine

Sung Po-jen must have had someone in mind when he wrote this poem. I wonder if it wasn't Li Pai, the poet of wine, who drowned, so the story goes, trying to embrace the moon in the waters of the Yangtze.

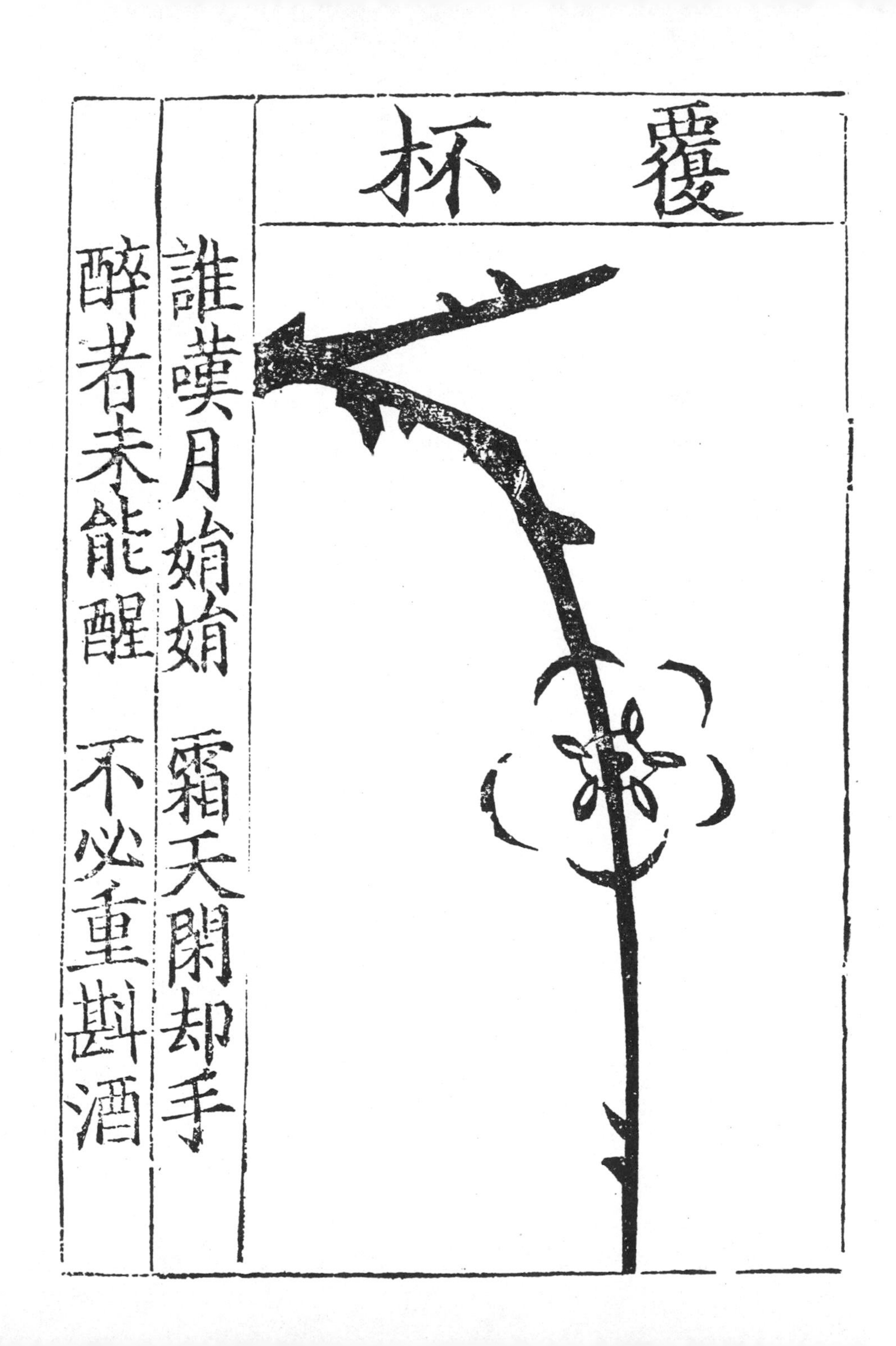
覆杯
誰嘆月娟娟　霜天閑却手
醉者未能醒　不必重斟酒

53 *Mien*

the *yen,* the *pi,* the *ts'ui, hsi,* and *hsuan*
twelve strands distinguish a king
adorned with pendants of jade
five colors to honor Chengchou

The *mien* was a flat-topped hat worn by emperors and high-ranking officials. The first line lists five types. The *yen* was worn at sacrifices to former kings, the *pi* at sacrifices to one's father, the *ts'ui* at sacrifices to the rivers and mountains of the four directions, the *hsi* at sacrifices to the gods of the soil and grain and the five household spirits, and the *hsuan* at the many minor sacrifices. Jade beads hung along the front edge of these hats on five, seven, nine, or twelve colored silk strands. The number depended on the wearer's status, with twelve reserved for kings and emperors. The use of five colors (black, white, red, blue, and yellow) began with the Chou dynasty, whose eastern capital was at Chengchou near the modern city of Loyang.

冕

衮鷩毳希玄　君尊十二旒

璪取玉以文　五采宗成周

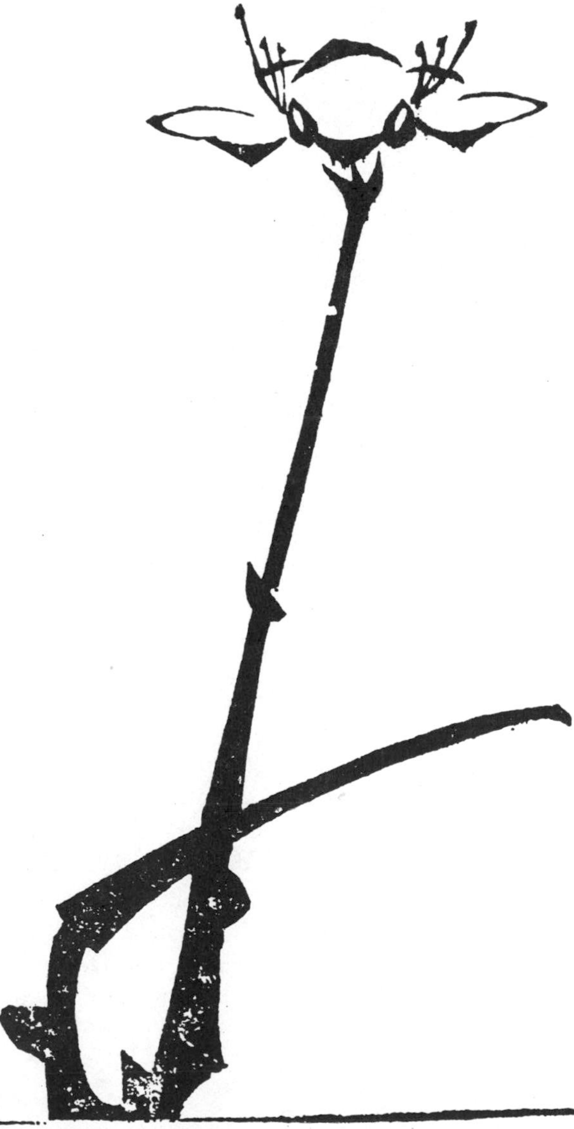

54 *Helmet*

on the shoulders mail lies cold
reminding us the plains aren't ours
when will we sweep border dust
another helmet looks toward Heaven

The helmet consisted of a peaked cap with flaps that hung down the sides and back of the neck. The cap was usually made of metal, and the flaps were made of beaten leather or finely linked chains of mail. When the *Guide* was written, the Mongols had just wrested the vast Yellow River and Huai River floodplains from the Jurchen tribe. A century earlier, the Jurchen had seized them from the Chinese, who then retreated south of the Yangtze to Hangchou. The Son of Heaven's inability and unwillingness to retake the plains and drive the barbarians back beyond the old borders was a source of great disappointment to his followers. Their hopes were finally crushed in 1276, when the Mongols completed their conquest of China.

胄

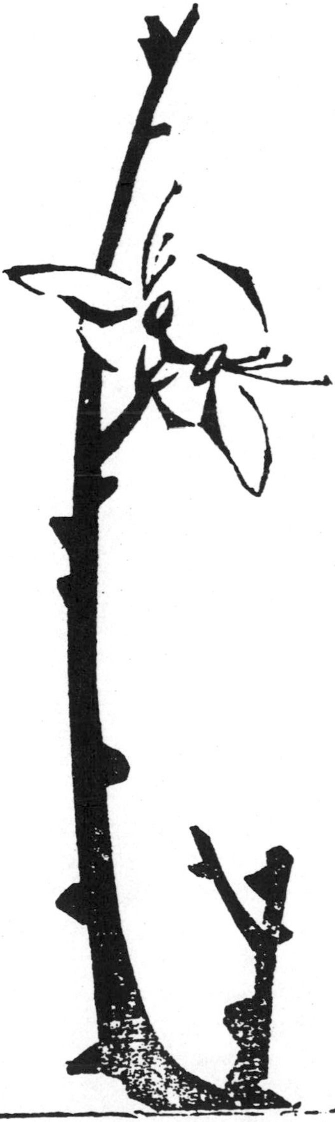

秀鐵壓肩寒　中原思未報
何日掃邊塵　別累朝天帽

55 *Pair of Peaches*

Emperor Wu wished to be immortal
the Queen Mother came down from Heaven
with peaches that took thousands of years
imagine stealing three

The Queen Mother of the West, Hsi-wang-mu, was the name of the chief divinity of the Kunlun Mountains in Central Asia. In addition to various magic powers, she possessed the elixir of immortality, which she dispensed in the form of peaches that ripened once every 3,000 years. Although she has been variously identified with Arabia's Queen of Sheba and the Greek goddess Hera, the Chinese describe her as having the tail of a panther and the teeth of a tiger. During the Chou dynasty, King Mu visited her at her palace in northern Afghanistan, and she returned the favor 800 years later, when she visited Emperor Wu of the Han dynasty and brought with her seven peaches. She presented four to the emperor and kept three for herself. No Chinese emperor spent more time or money trying to attain the Taoist goal of immortality, and numerous stories about Emperor Wu's quest appeared in subsequent centuries. In one, his advisor, Tung-fang Shuo, steals three of the Queen Mother's peaches, but they fall out of his robe as he prepares to leave. And in another version, a dwarf presented at court brags to Tung-fang that he also stole three of the Queen Mother's immortal fruits.

並桃

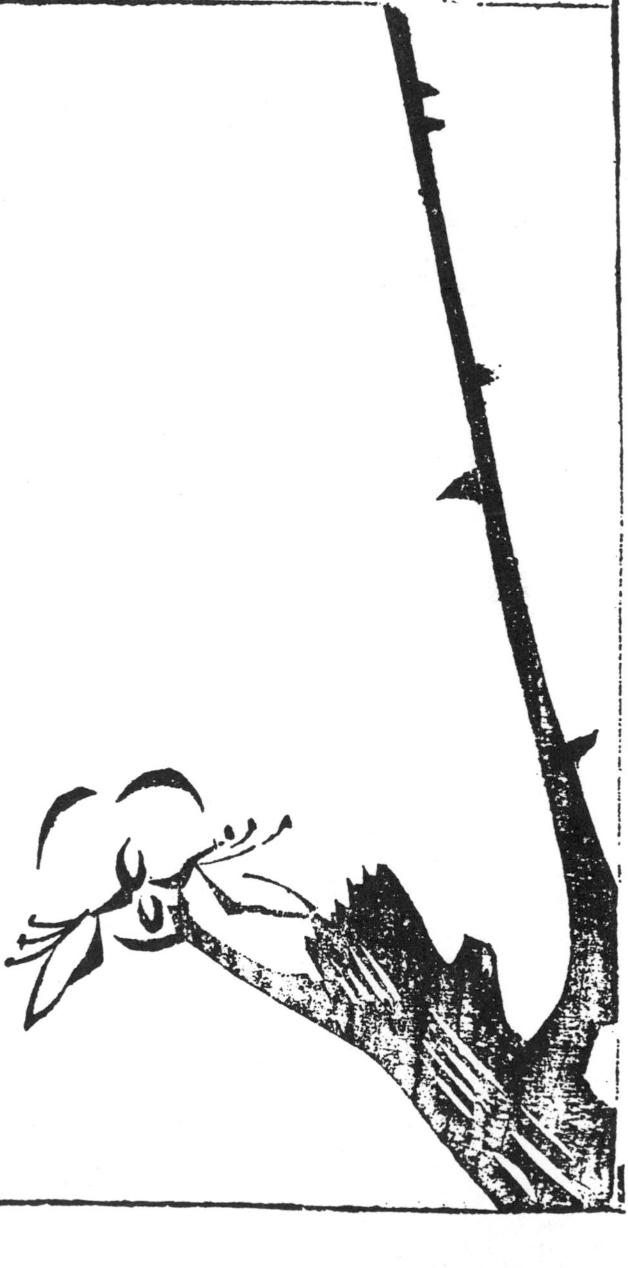

漢帝欲成仙　王毋從天下

結實動千年　三偷尤可詫

56 *Pair of Lichees*

silken shells on golden branches
summer fruit with new green leaves
Yu-chen wanted something luscious
she didn't care if couriers suffered

The opaque, white fruit of the lichee is enclosed by a thin red shell. A semitropical fruit, it grows only in China's southernmost provinces. Yang Yu-chen was Emperor Hsuan-tsung's favorite concubine, and she was so fond of lichees it took several hundred relay riders to keep her supplied during the summer, when the fruit was in season. When the An Lu-shan Rebellion broke out in A.D. 756, Yu-chen was blamed for Hsuan-tsung's extravagant use of public funds and his inattention to government. She was strangled during the emperor's flight from the capital and buried at the side of the road. Her grave sixty kilometers west of Sian still attracts visitors.

雙荔

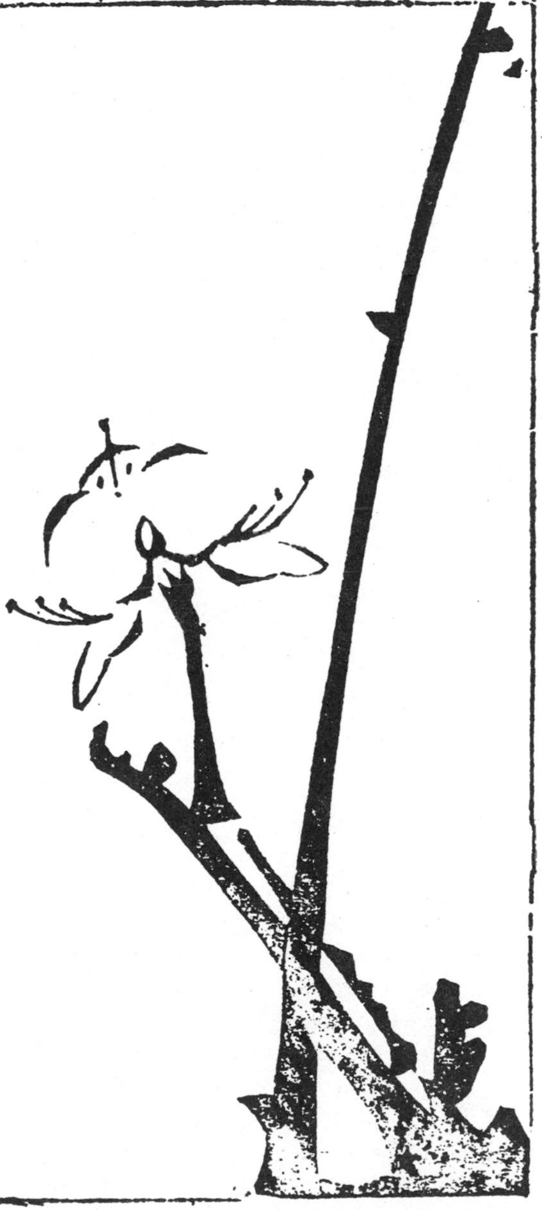

縐殼爛緗枝　夏菓收新緑

玉真望甘鮮　不管郵兵哭

57 *Phoenix Facing Heaven*

beholding light high in the sky
a gentleman thinks of order
if he fails to sing at dawn
let him feel ashamed

The phoenix only appears when a virtuous ruler sits on the throne and order prevails in the world. The Son of Heaven traditionally conducted the business of court before dawn. All senior officials in the capital were expected to attend, and those with complaints or recommendations were encouraged to present them to the throne. A poem by the Han dynasty poet Chia Yi lamenting the death of Ch'u Yuan, who was exiled for his unwelcome advice, seems to have inspired the opening line: "the phoenix soars high in the sky / beholding the light of virtue it descends."

鳳朝天

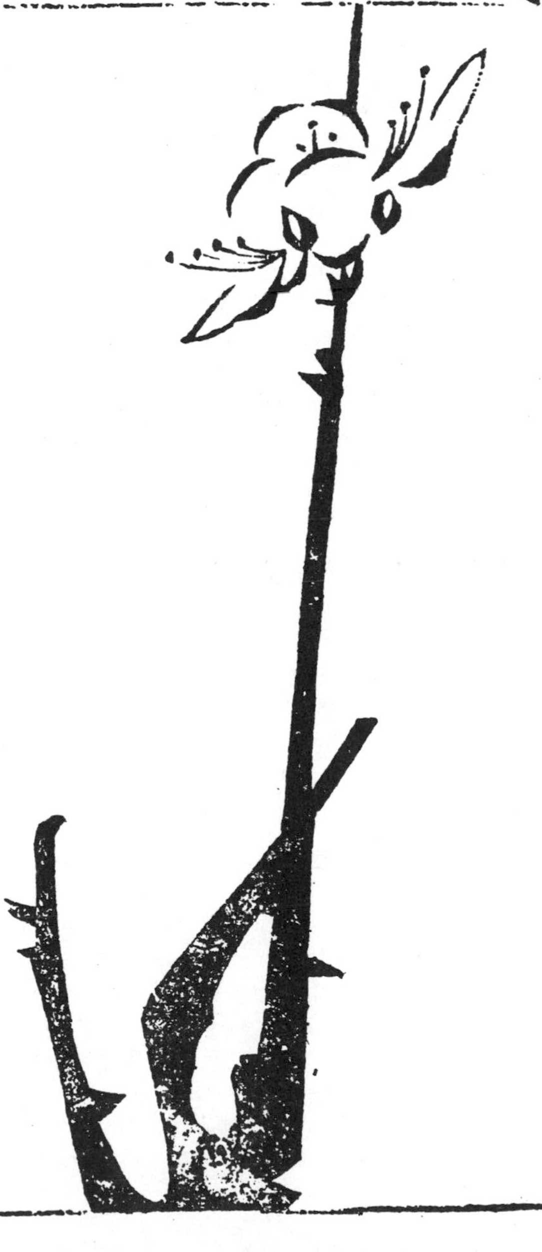

覽輝千仞高　君子思在治

朝陽如不鳴　敢言當自愧

58 *Spider on a Web*

its weavings come from Heaven
hanging nets under painted eaves
more clever than a silkworm
alas no help to man

In ancient China, sumptuary regulations restricted the use of painted designs under eaves and inside houses to the dwellings of the nobility. The Chinese date the invention of silk to the time of the Yellow Emperor, or around 2600 B.C. One day his wife, Lei-tsu, was drinking tea, when a silkworm cocoon fell from a mulberry branch into her cup. While trying to remove it, she began unreeling the cocoon and discovered the secret of making silk. The traditional attribution notwithstanding, silkworms appear in China's archaeological record at least 2,000 years before the Yellow Emperor's time. The spider, meanwhile, meets Chuang-tzu's qualification for attaining old age by being useless to mankind (*Chuangtzu,* 4).

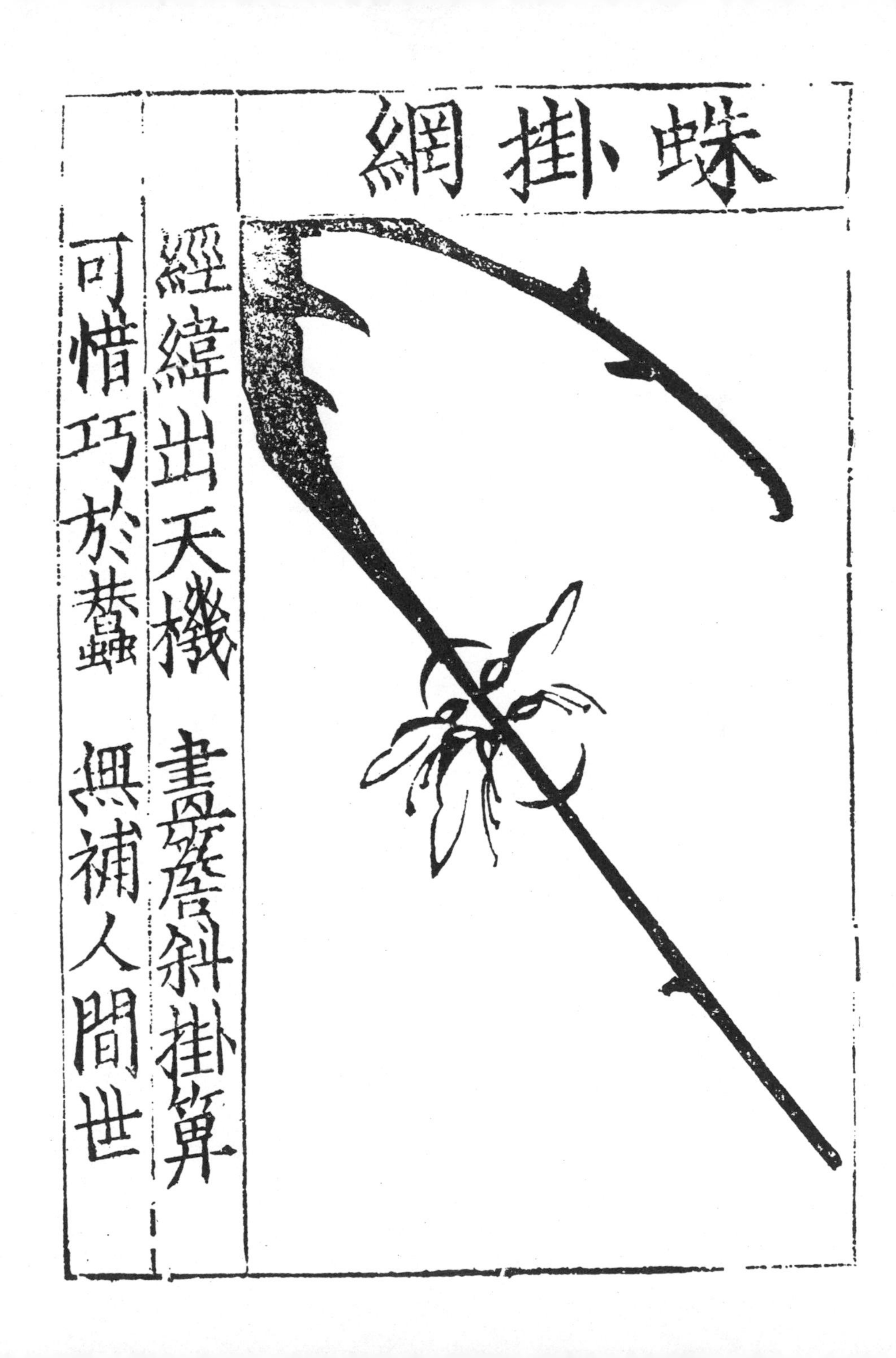
蛛掛網
經緯出天機
晝簷斜掛算
可惜巧於蠹
無補人間世

59 *Fisherman's Hat*

anchored out among the gulls
cold rain lashes a hat of leaves
unconceerned with fearsome waves
now he knows the joys of water

The fisherman's hat is made of bamboo leaves attached to a frame of bamboo strips. Ever since Confucius attributed kindness to the person who loves mountains and wisdom to the person who loves water (*Analects,* 6), the love of water has been synonymous with detachment from social convention and the life of the vagabond or recluse.

漁笠

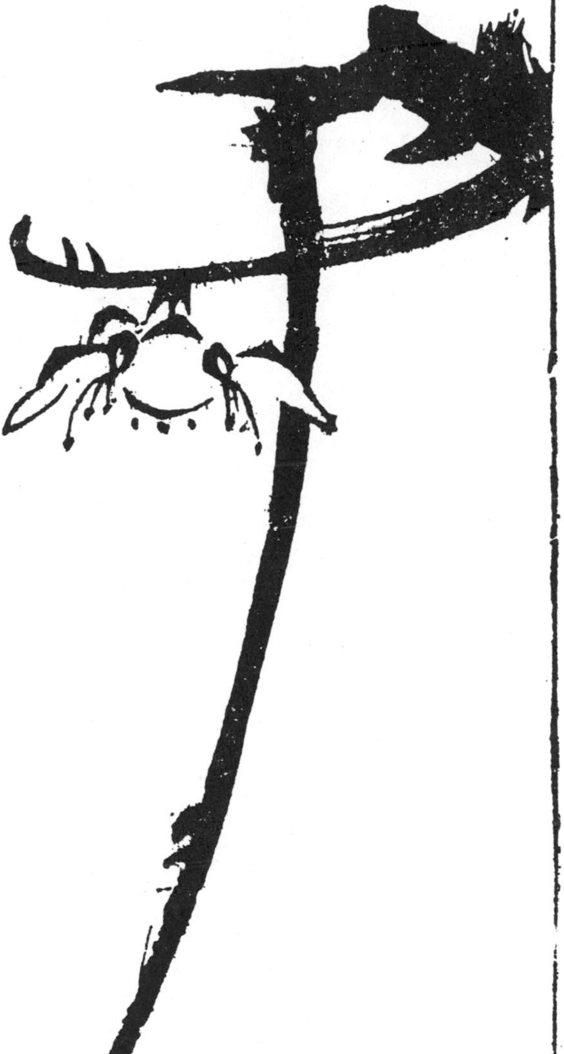

艤艇白鷗邊
寒雨敲青箬
駭浪不回頭
方識江湖樂

60 *Bear Paw*

subtlest of the eight rare dishes
it never fills a common stomach
man alas wants his meat
and wants his fish as well

Along with such metaphorical dishes as dragon liver and phoenix marrow, bear paws were included among the eight delicacies reserved for special banquets. Mencius said, "I love fish, and I love bear paws. If I can't have both, I'll give up fish for bear paws. I love life, and I love righteousness. If I can't have both, I'll give up life for righteousness." (*Mencius,* 6.1)

熊掌

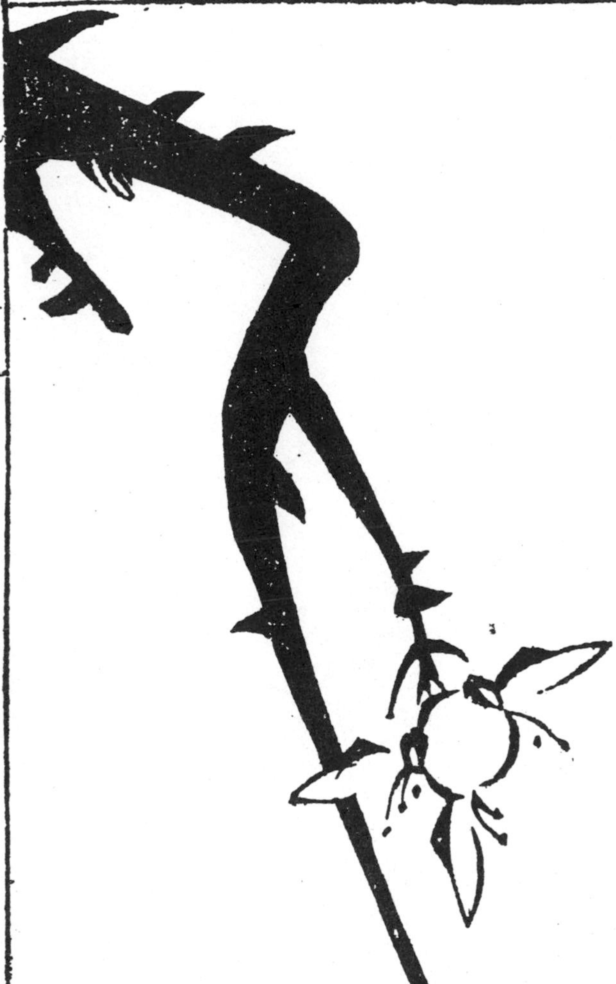

八珍風味清　藜賜豈曾識

堪嗤嘗臠人　欲與魚兼得

61 *Flying Creature Stings a Flower*

a flower's scent brings butterflies
something else arrives as well
vanity that knows no shame
pain born from desire

Here, the flower represents narcissistic love, while the flying creature, apparently a bee, is meant to remind us of sexual predators attracted by the flower's public display of beauty. Desire is one of greatest dangers to those who strive to cultivate tranquility. The *Kuoyu* says, "Righteousness is the source of profit. Desire is the origin of regret."

飛蟲刺花

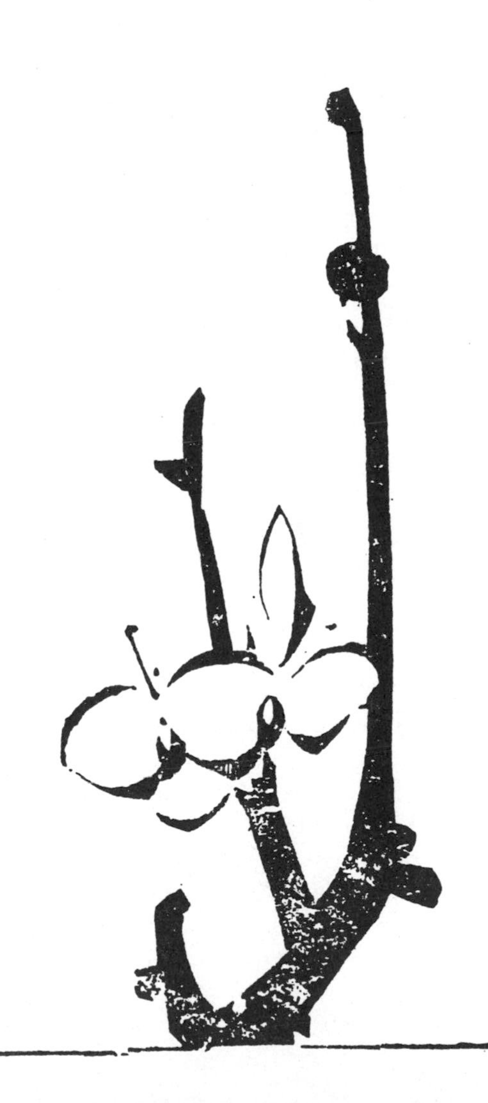

花香尋引蝶　非蝶亦飛來
顧影不知恥　良爲貪者哀

62 *Lone Goose Calling to the Moon*

a letter tied to a goose's foot
gained Tzu-ch'ing his freedom
even though he tricked the Khan
the ages call him honest

In 105 B.C. Su Tzu-ch'ing (Su Wu) was sent as an envoy to the Hsiung-nu, who occupied parts of northwest China and threatened trade on the Silk Road. But when Su refused to acknowledge the superiority of the nomadic kingdom, the Hsiung-nu khan made him his prisoner. Even when peaceful relations were established twenty years later, the khan continued to deny knowledge of Su Tzu-ch'ing's whereabouts. Finally, Su Tzu-ch'ing managed to get word of his existence to the new Chinese envoy, together with a plan for his release. Su suggested the envoy tell the khan that during a hunt the Chinese emperor shot a wild goose and found a letter from Su Tzu-ch'ing attached to its foot. When the envoy did as Su suggested, the khan had no choice but to order Su's release.

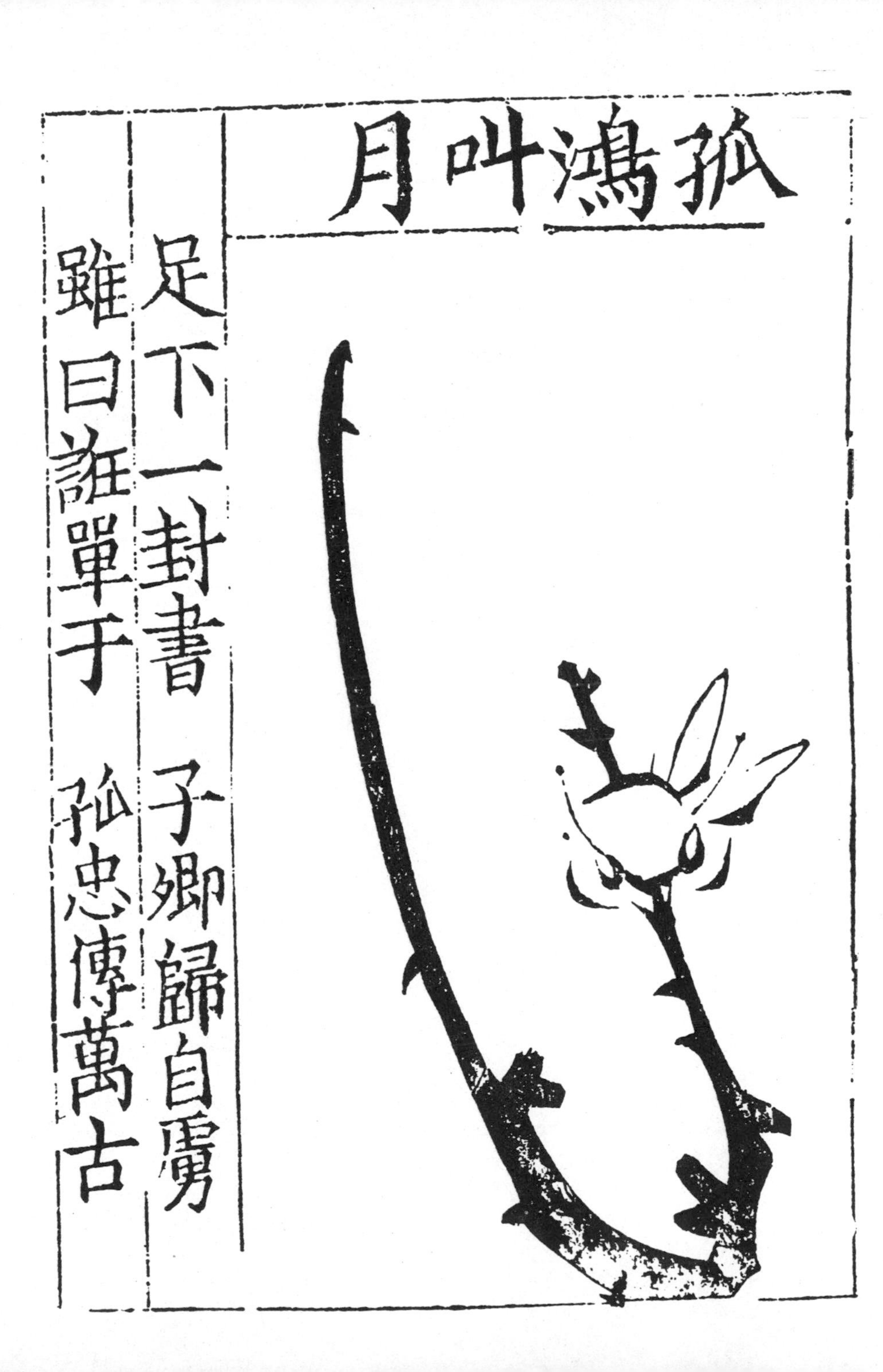
孤鴻叫月
足下一封書　子卿歸自虜
雖曰誑單于　孤忠傳萬古

63 *Turtle Feet*

a shell full of holes
or freedom from knives
better to hide beneath lily pads
to swim in bliss for a thousand years

Turtles were thought to live thousands of years and to possess knowledge of the future. To access this knowledge, the Chinese drilled and heated the upper shell and lower plastron and interpreted the resulting cracks to predict coming events. Once, when Chuang-tzu was fishing along the P'u River, two emissaries from the state of Ch'u approached him and said, "Our lord wishes to entrust administration of his realm to you." Without bothering to put down his fishing pole, Chuang-tzu replied, "I've heard that your king has a 3,000-year-old turtle shell he keeps on his ancestral altar. Do you think the turtle would rather be dead and have its shell so honored or be alive and dragging its tail in the mud? Leave me be. I'd rather drag my tail in the mud" (*Chuangtzu,* 17).

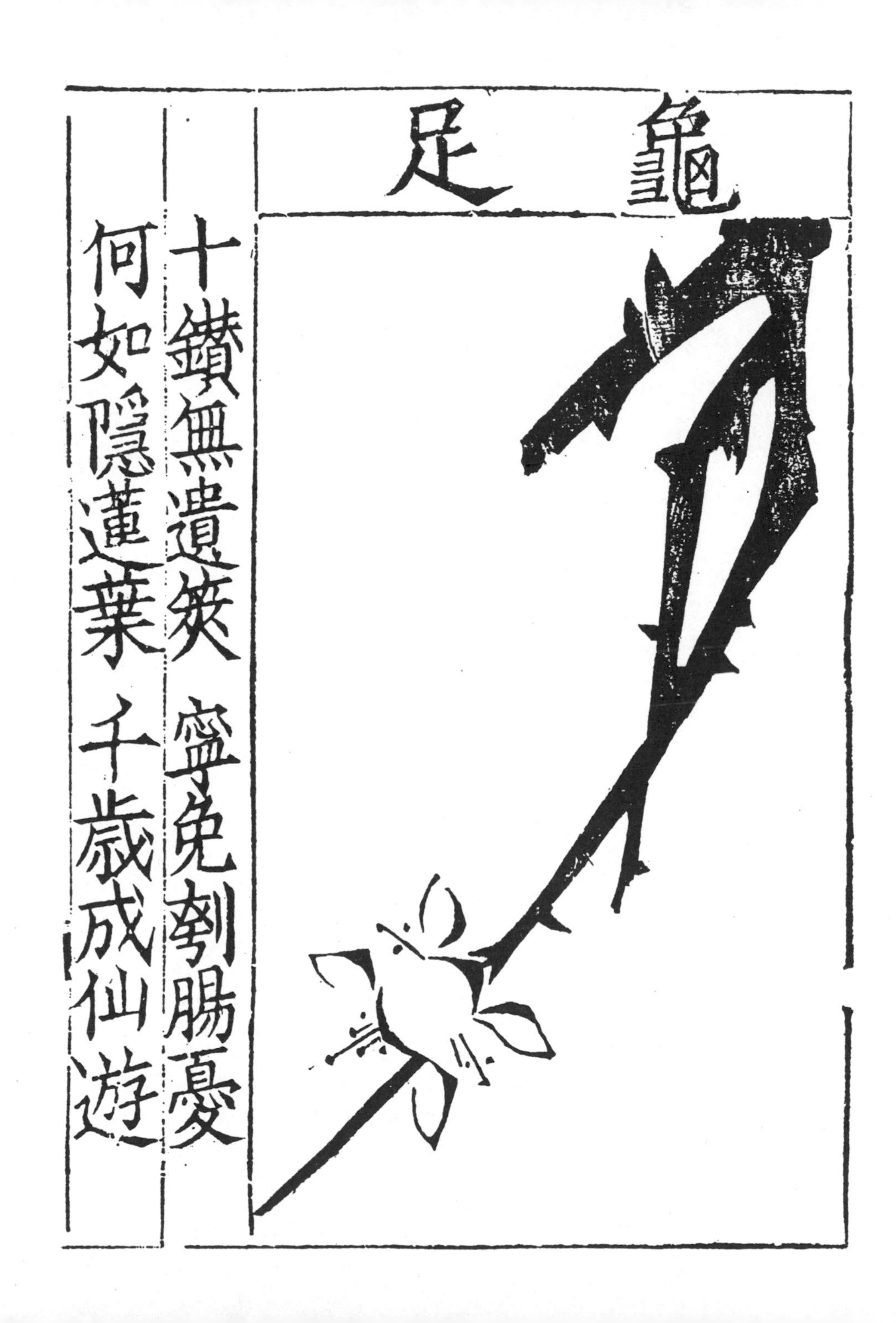

龜足
十鑚無遺筴 寧免刳腸憂
何如隱蓮葉 千歲成仙游

64 *Dragon Claws*

farmers look for rainbows
can't stay a pond creature for long
K'ung-ming sleeping near Lungchung
made the emperor bow

Referring to one of China's earliest political heroes, Mencius said, "The people looked to Emperor T'ang as they did to rainbows during a drought" (*Mencius,* 1.2). Dragons are thought to control the rain and are said to live in deep water. Hence, a pond isn't likely to hold a young dragon for long. Men of great talent are also likened to dragons, and the last two lines are about Chu-ko Liang, who was also called K'ung-ming. In the third century A.D., Chu-ko Liang lived as a hermit near the village of Lungchung in Hupei province. People said he was a sleeping dragon capable of great things. Liu Pei, the future emperor of the Shu-Han dynasty, resolved to see for himself. Twice Liu Pei visited Chu-ko Liang's hut, and twice Chu-ko Liang declined to get up to open the door. Only on the third visit did the two men finally meet. Later, as Liu Pei's chief advisor, Chu-ko Liang left no doubt that he was one of the greatest strategists the world has ever known. On one occasion, he drove off an army of 200,000 with a handful of men and his zither.

龍爪

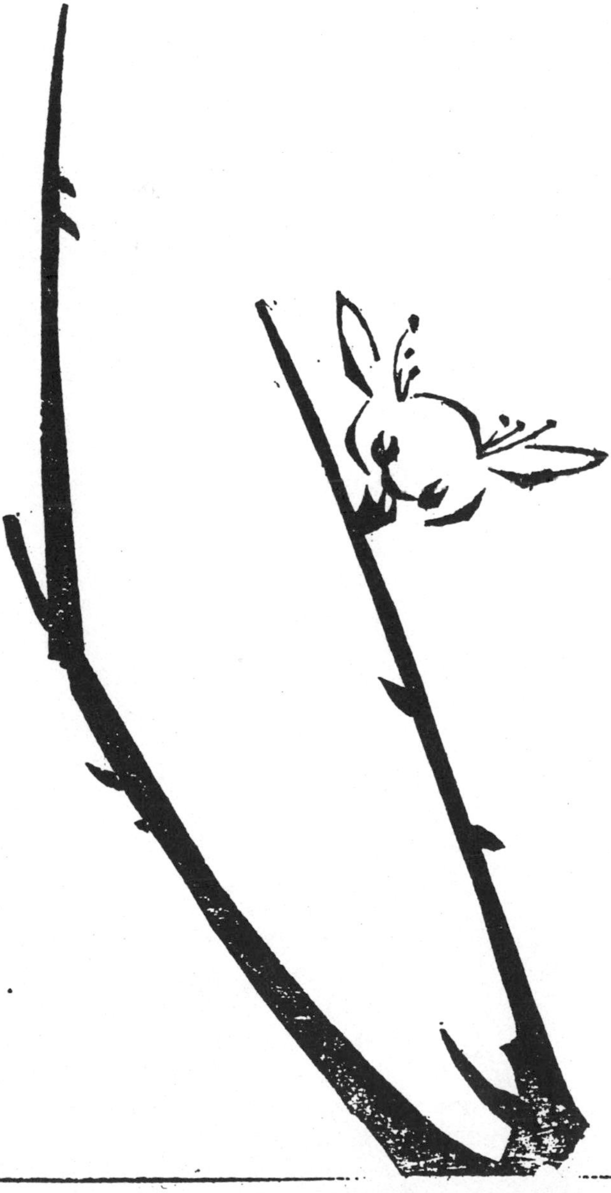

蒼生望雲霓　難作池中物

孔明卧隆中　天子勢亦屈

65 *Rooster on a Tree Flapping Its Wings*

in the cold wings flap three times
wind and rain don't change
who gets up to dance
true men don't stay in bed

In a poem in the *Book of Songs* titled "Wind and Rain," a cock crows in the cold three times, each time reminding the listener of a friend and reminding him not to let his love change. Tsu T'i served as a general in the early years of the fourth century A.D. and never avoided a chance for adventure. When he was younger and serving in the capital of Loyang, he slept under the same blanket with his comrade-in-arms, Liu K'un. Whenever they heard a cock crow, even if it was the middle of the night, they both got up and danced.

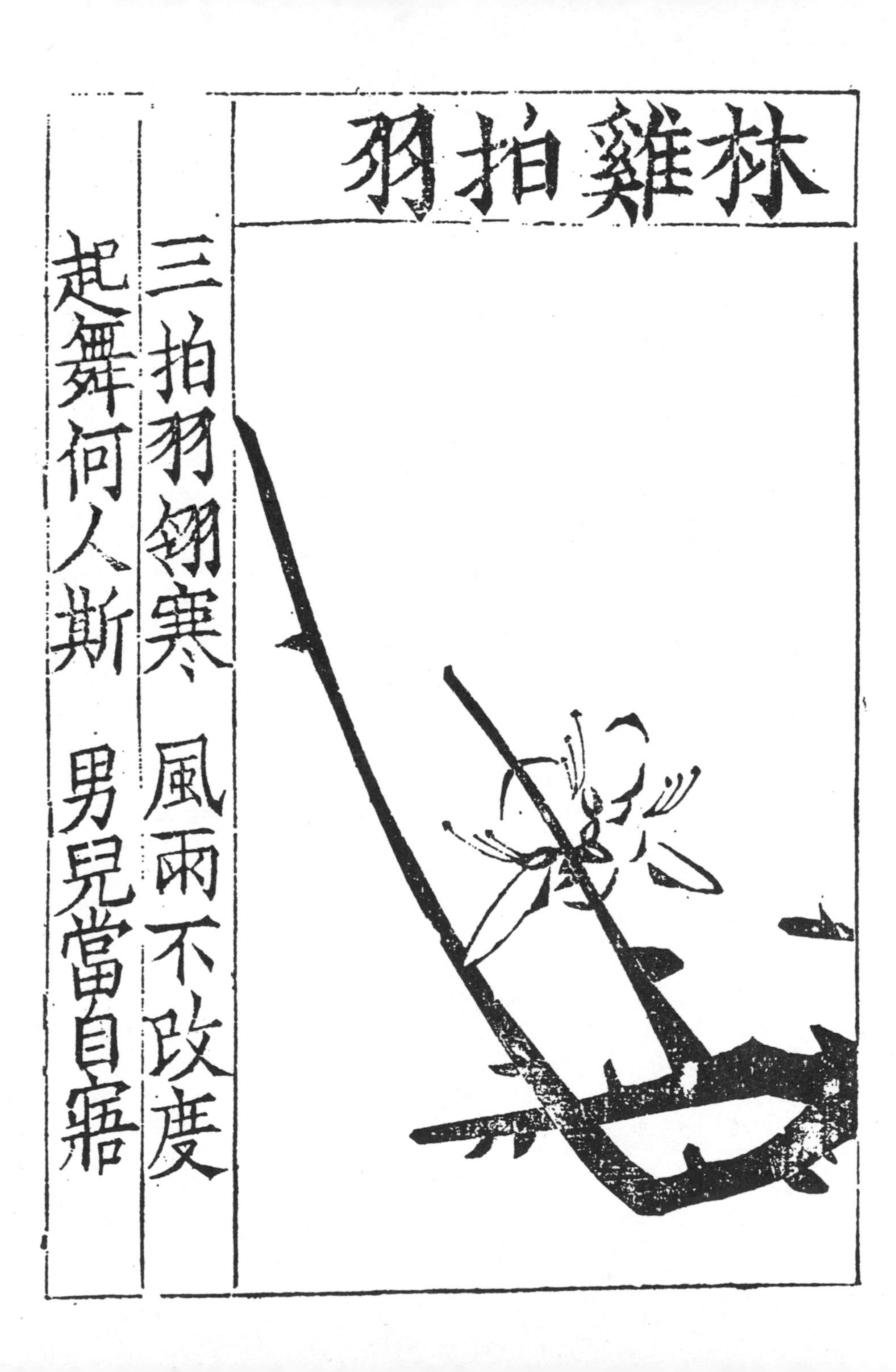
林雞拍羽
三拍羽翎寒 風雨不改度
起舞何人斯 男兒當自寤

66 *Crane on a Pine Crying to Heaven*

waking from a Red Cliff dream
black robe soaked with rain
trying to reach Heaven's ear
it stands atop a pine

The eleventh-century poet Su Tung-p'o wrote two poems about his visit to a place on the Yangtze called Red Cliff—not the scene of the famous battle upriver from Wuhan, but a place of the same name downriver. In the second of these poems, Su sees a crane fly overhead, and later that night in a dream the crane turns into a black-robed Taoist immortal. The Chinese believe the crane lives hundreds of years and is the transformed embodiment of a person who has attained the Taoist goal of immortality. Although its body is white, the crane's tail feathers and wing tips are black. In a poem in the *Book of Songs* titled "Cry of the Crane," the chance of a person who cultivates the Tao in obscurity coming to the attention of the emperor is likened to a crane's cry being heard in Heaven.

松鶴唳天

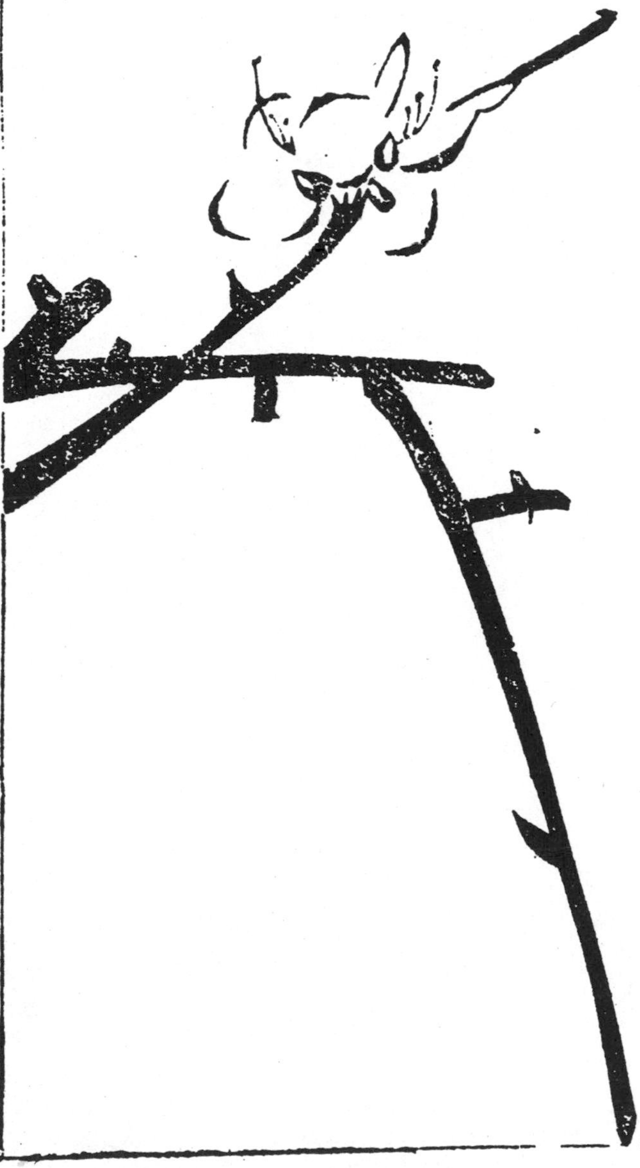

赤壁夢醒時　雨灑玄裳濕

聲欲聞于天　故向松梢立

67 *New Lily Pads in Pouring Rain*

small pond newly green
pads of floating jade-like coins
in the rain ten thousand pearls
await a clever wife to string

"Clever wife" is another name for the tailor bird, which builds its nest with great skill out of next to nothing. Here, Sung Po-jen calls on it to fashion a necklace from raindrops.

新荷濺雨

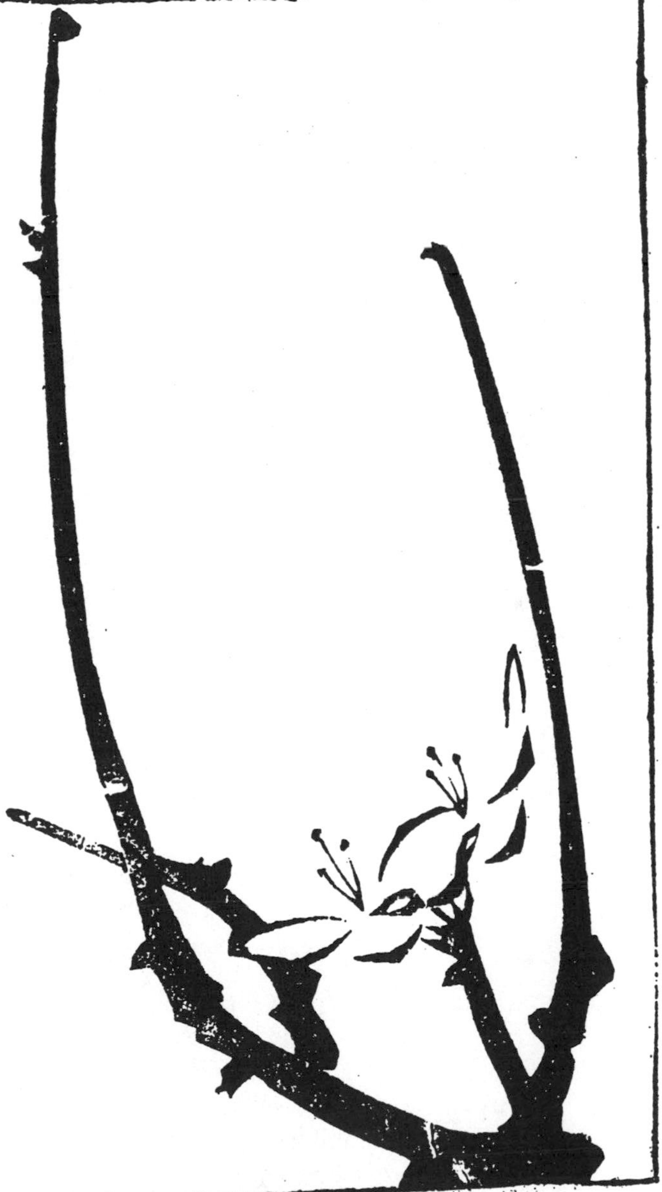

新緑小池沼　田田浮翠錢

雨中珠萬顆　巧婦其能穿

68 *Old Chrysanthemum with Coat of Frost*

no Yuan-ming for ages now
yellow flowers bloom in vain
once the Blue Girl looms above
winter perfume doesn't linger

The chrysanthemum, which blooms in the ninth lunar month, is celebrated as a symbol of old age. It was the favorite flower of the fourth-century poet T'ao Yuan-ming, who immortalized its yellow petals in his poetry and infused them in his wine. The Jade Maiden of the Blue Sky is the spirit that controls the frost and snow. The shorter form of her name, used here, is another name for the ninth month.

老菊披霜

世久無淵明　黃花為誰好

青女自凌威　寒香未容老

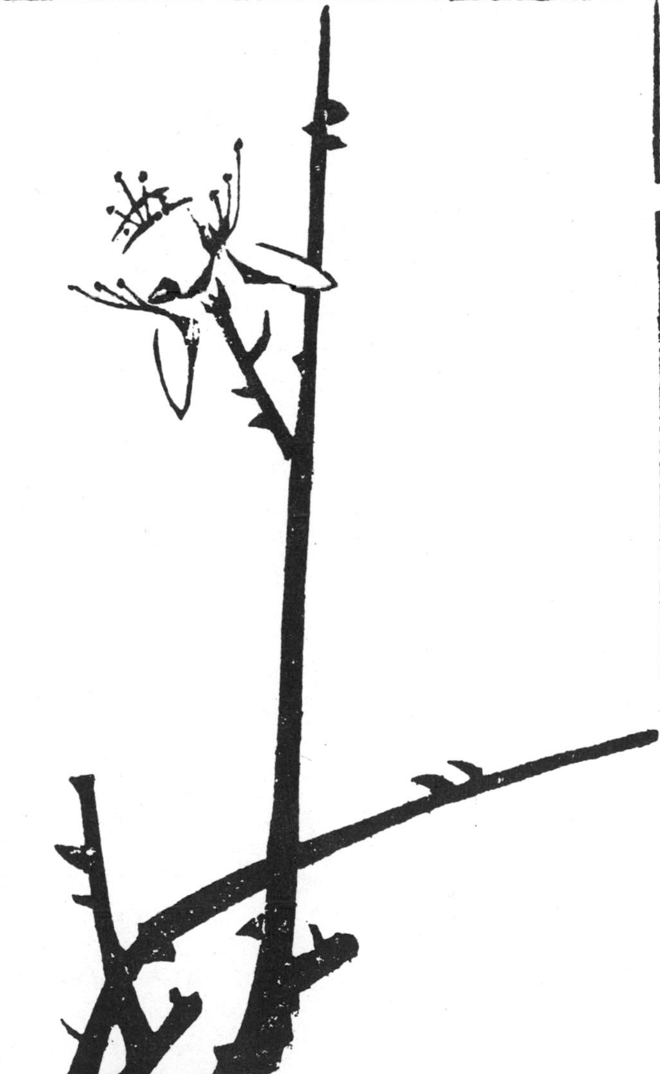

69 *Zither*

Tien was different from the others
setting down his zither he rose
along the river peaks of green
the spirits of the Hsiang are lonely

Tien was the personal name of Tseng Hsi, a disciple of Confucius. One day Confucius asked several of his students what they desired most. All replied that they wanted positions of authority, except Tien. When it was his turn, he put down his zither, rose to his feet, and said he would like to go with a group of young men to the countryside in spring, wash away the dust of the past year in the river, dry off in the breeze at the rain-dance altar, and return home singing. Confucius said he agreed with Tien (*Analects,* 11).

The last two lines recall a poem titled "Drum and Zither of the Hsiang River Spirits" by the eighth-century poet Ch'ien Ch'i. His poem includes the refrain, "The song is over the players gone / along the river peaks of green." The song is about Emperor Shun's two wives, who lived some 4,000 years ago and who often entertained their husband with their zithers. When he died, they drowned themselves in the Hsiang River. Ever since then they have been worshiped as the river's twin spirits. Their grave is on a small island in the middle of Tungting Lake, which is formed by the Hsiang and several other rivers, and which in turn empties into the Yangtze. China's first great poet, Ch'u Yuan, also drowned himself in a nearby tributary of the Hsiang in the third century B.C., and no doubt Sung Po-jen had his spirit in mind as well.

瑟

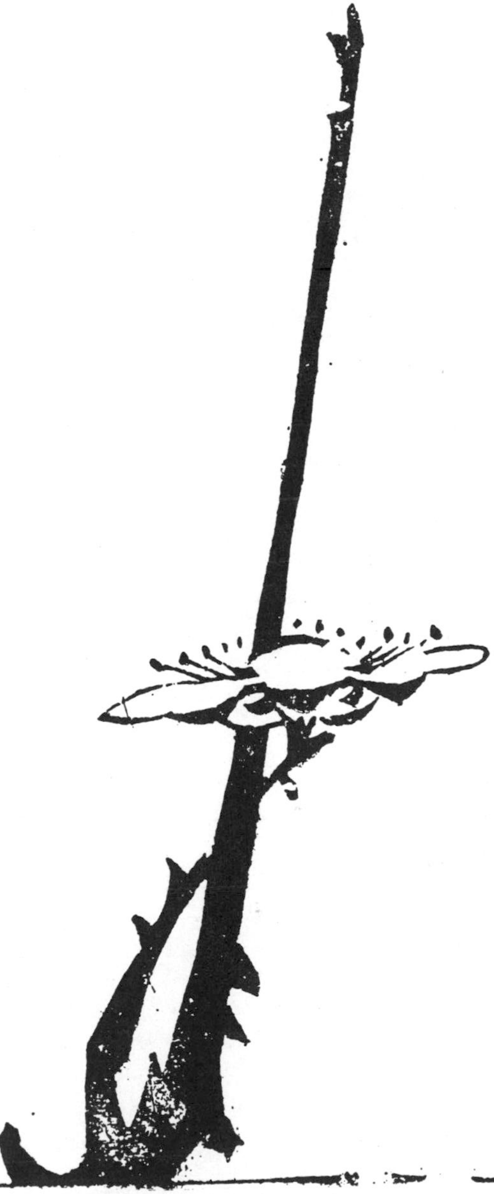

點異二三子　鏗爾舍而作

江上數峰青　湘靈徒寂寞

70 *Drum*

boom-boom blends with voice and flute
mud-filled drumsticks though are lacking
laughable so out of place
a drum of cloth at Thunder Gate

In the fifth century B.C., King Kou Chien of the state of Yueh ordered construction of a huge drum to outdo the neighboring state of Wu, which had earlier defeated Yueh. The drum, made from the hide of a giant bull, was nine meters in circumference. Its sound was said to carry all the way to the Chou dynasty capital of Loyang, a distance of 1,000 kilometers. Before it was destroyed in the fourth century A.D., the drum was kept at Thunder Gate in Yueh's ancient capital of Shaohsing. Drumsticks for such large drums were made of woven bamboo and filled with mud. The Han dynasty scholar Wang Tsun once described a fool as someone who beats a cloth drum below Thunder Gate.

皷

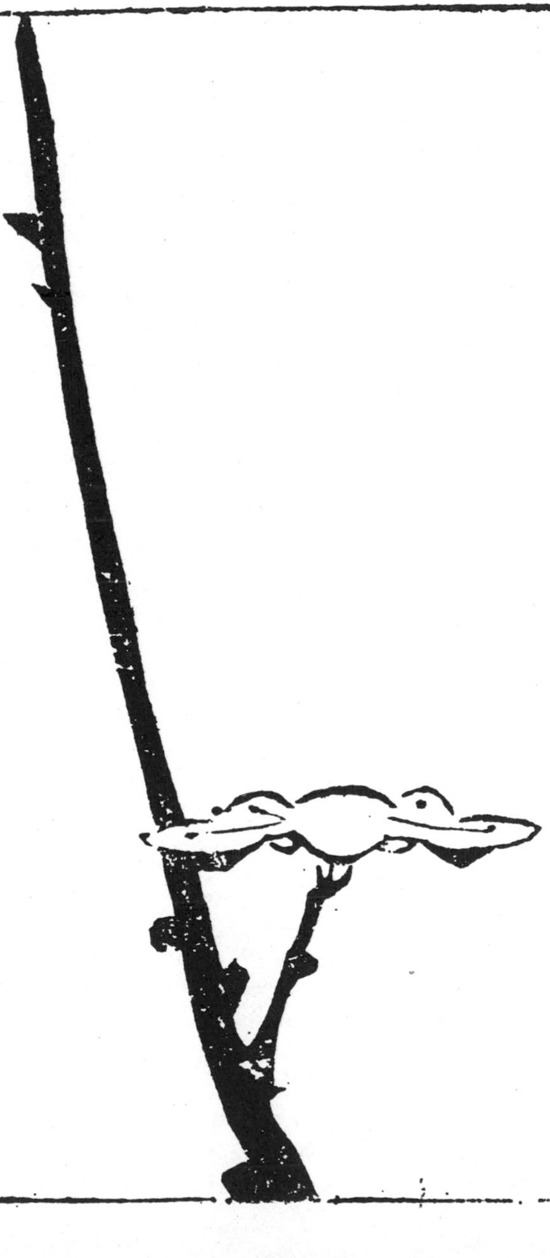

鼕鼕和歌管　蕢桴無復存

堪笑不知量　以布過雷門

71 *Bee Waist*

a warming breeze on purple paths
beehives in the mountain deep
if their honey isn't tasted
flowers give their hearts in vain

The purple paths are those of the capital, down which royalty rode in splendor. The warm breeze of spring suggests the beginning of a new reign and the invitation for men of virtue to come out of retirement and present themselves at court. Hermits in China still make their huts out of mud. Here, "beehives" refers to their places of solitude and not, as it might seem, to places of activity. "Bee waist" refers to an error in versification where the second and fourth sounds in a line have the same tone —as in the last line of this verse.

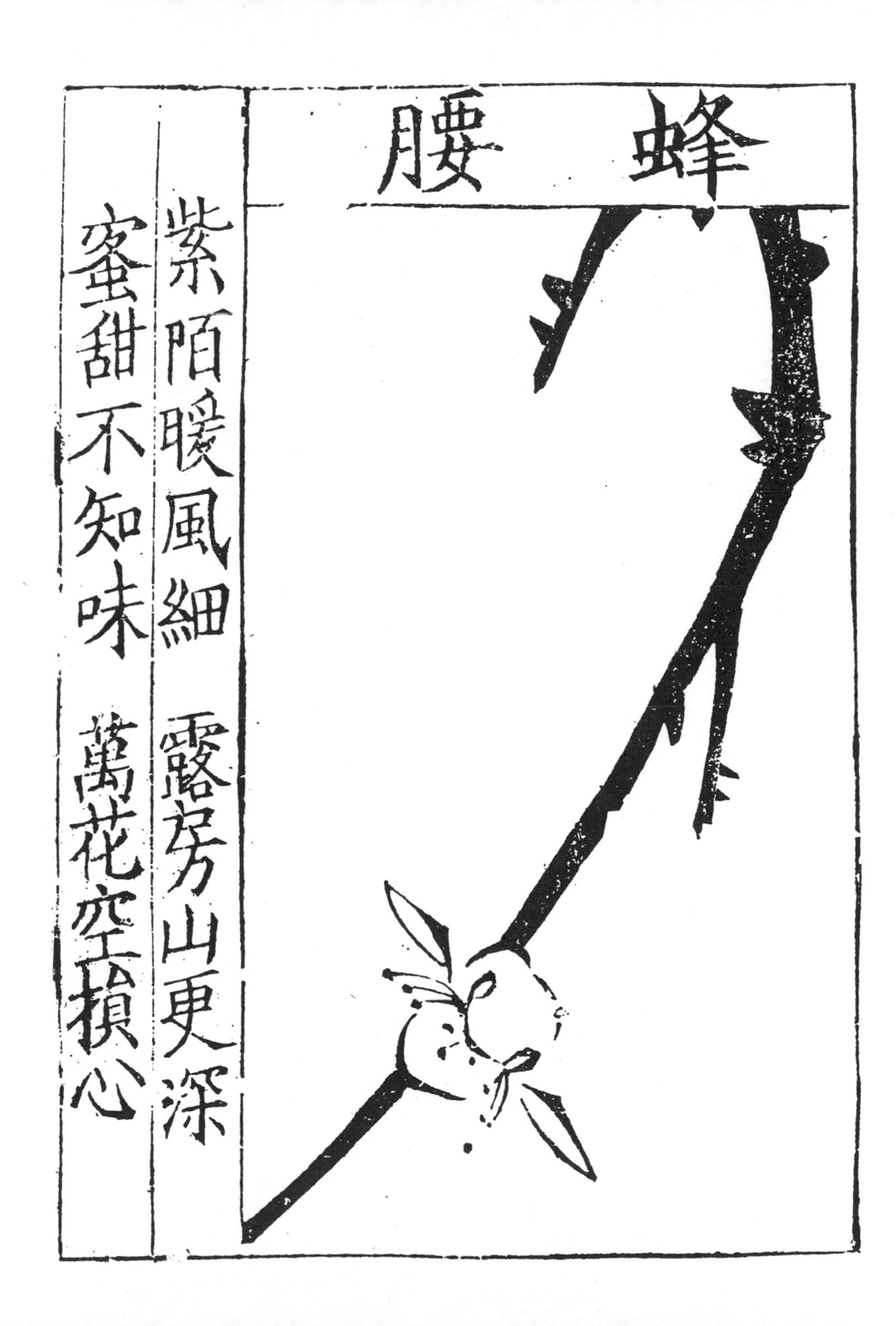

蜂腰
紫陌暖風細　露房山更深
蜜甜不知味　萬花空損心

72 *Swallowtail*

east wind parts embroidered curtains
perches on a flower tip
where it finds false-hearted friends
it declines their painted beams

The east wind is the wind of success. In China, it blows in spring, which is also when swallows return with the promise of good fortune for the homes they choose for their nests. Embroidered curtains and painted beams refer to the homes of the rich. The poet Wu Kuan once wrote: "butterflies fill a branch in bloom / then leave when flowers fade / only swallows once again / return to the home that's poor."

燕尾

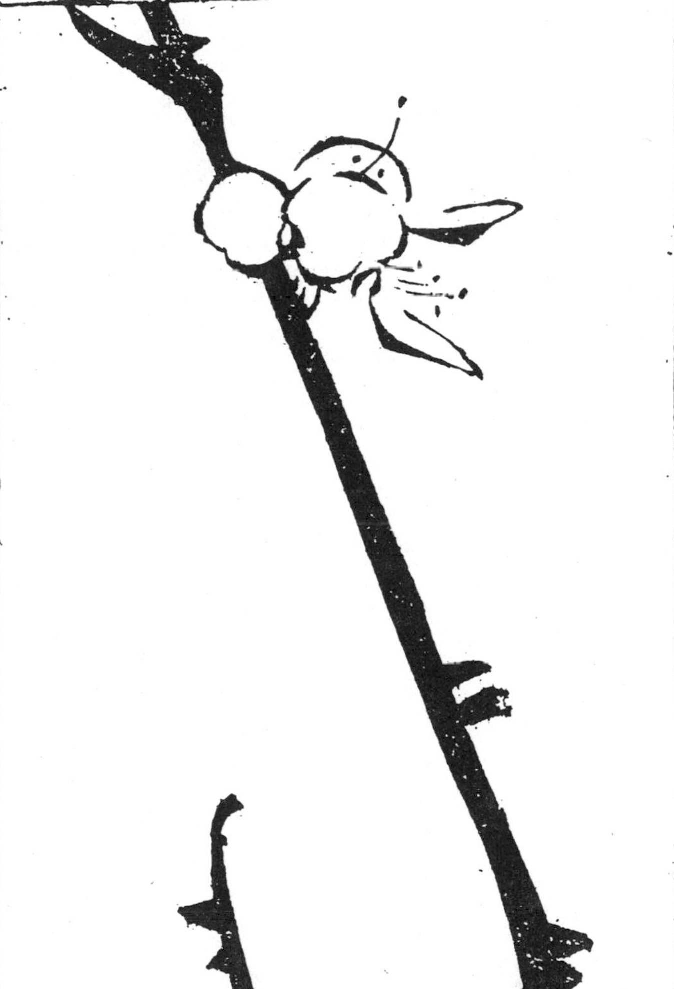

東風開繡簾　且向花梢立
主人忘舊交　雕梁不須入

73 *Frightened Gull Flapping Its Wings*

snowy wings on a sunny shore
the fisherman means no harm
scheming though can't be ignored
best for now to fly away

The Taoist philosopher Lieh-tzu tells this story: "There once was a young man who lived by the sea who loved seagulls. Whenever he walked along the shore, more than a hundred birds followed him. One day his father told him to catch a few and bring them back to keep as pets. The next day, when the young man went walking along the shore, not one seagull would approach him" (*Liehtzu,* 2).

驚鷗振翼

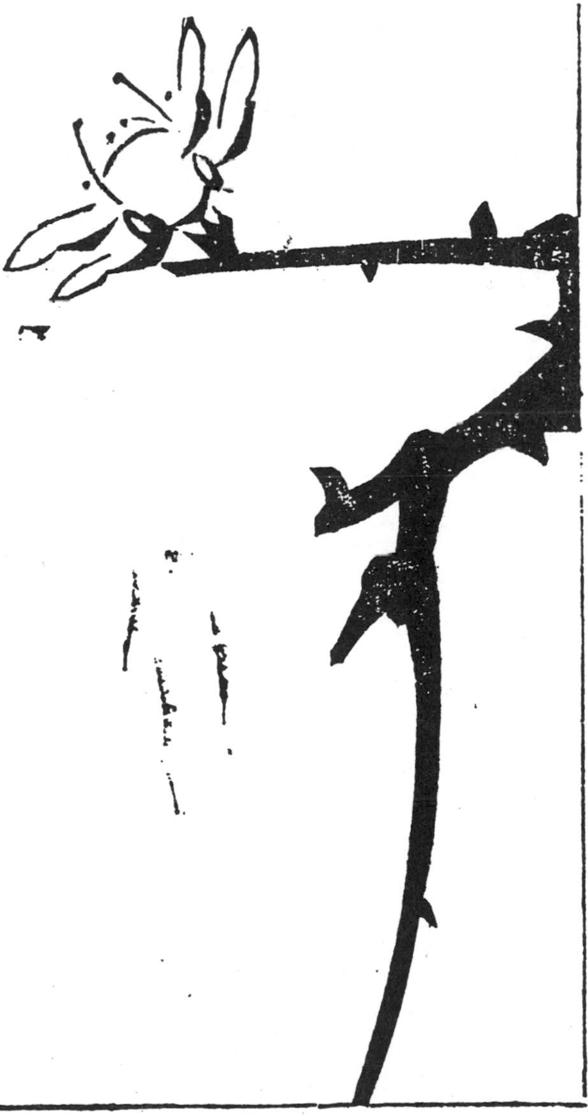

雪羽卧晴沙　漁人無可慮

機事亦難忘　不如且飛去

74 *Wheeling Hawk*

a bird of prey forgets its kind
it wheels and grabs a pigeon
feathered creatures share the sky
why this need to oppress the weak

The use of hawks and falcons for hunting is still common among the Mongols, Uighurs, and other ethnic groups who live in China's northern provinces. In addition to serving as emblems of authority, birds of prey also call to mind the rapaciousness of the powerful regarding the less fortunate.

野鶻翻身

很禽志所儔　翻身挈鳥雀

羽毛同所天　何苦強凌弱

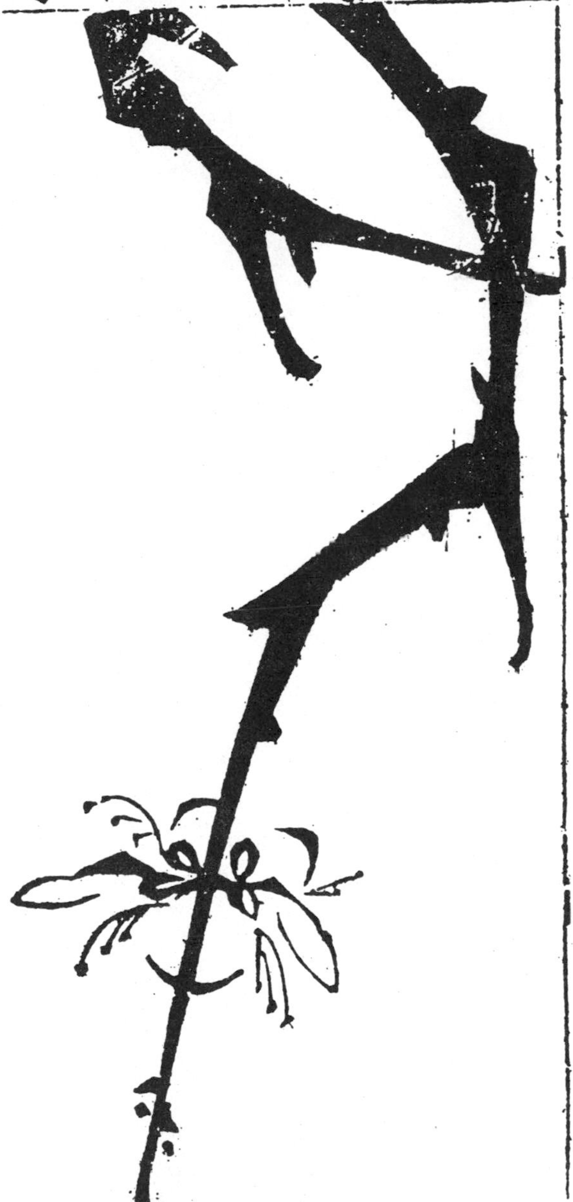

75 *Pondering the Next Step*

perilous are all worldly paths
advancing think of turning back
with every step a look behind
no more careless stumbles

The path to worldly success is not the path recommended by Confucius, Lao-tzu, or other Chinese sages. Concerning the ancient masters of the Tao, Lao-tzu says, "I describe them with reluctance / they were hesitant, as if crossing a river in winter / timid, as if worried about neighbors" (*Taoteching,* 15).

顧步

世道多巇嘘
進趨思退却
一步一回頭
庶無輕失脚

76 *Applying Makeup*

skilled at putting on powder and paint
seeing their likeness in a *ling* flower
supposing no one fought over beauty
would Hsi Shih smile

Bronze mirrors in the shape of the eight-petalled *ling* flower (see number 51) were popular in the Sung dynasty. Hsi Shih, one of ancient China's most famous beauties, was known for her constant frown, which many people thought contributed to her charm.

掩粧

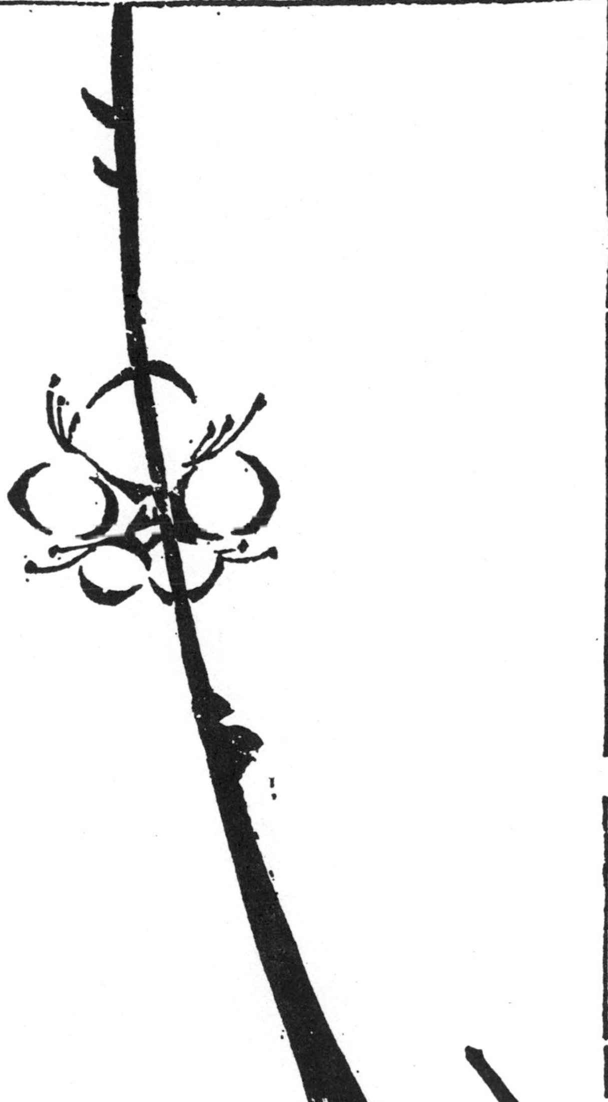

粉黛巧粧施　菱花還自照
底事不爭妍　又恐西施笑

77 *Clear Sky Crescent* Moon

a thousand miles no trace of clouds
a hook hangs in an azure sky
waxing waning without cease
mankind in bliss or pain

K'ang T'ing-chih's "Ode to the Moon" begins, "Before the terrace like a hanging mirror / beyond the curtain like a dangling hook."

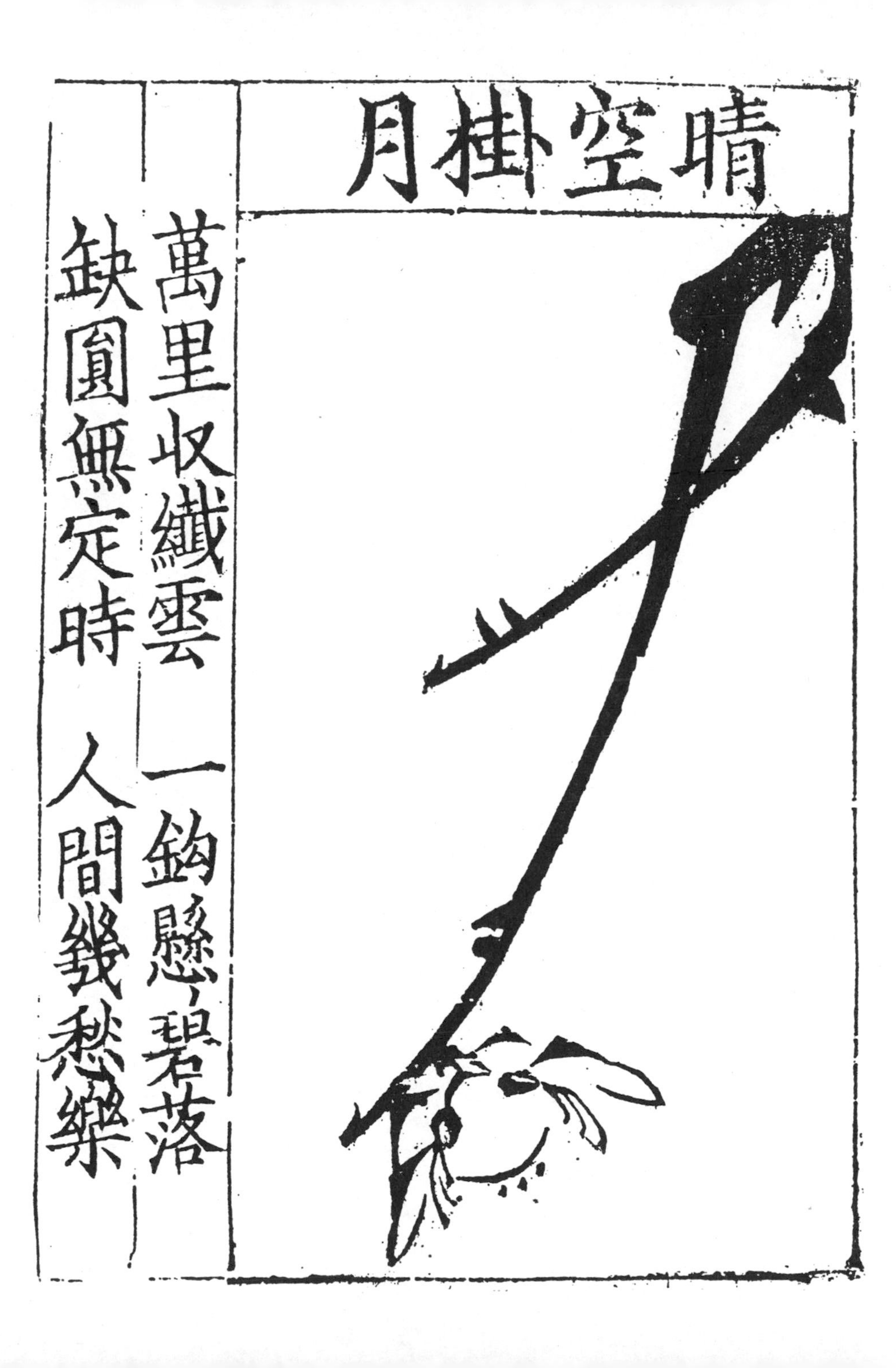
晴空掛月
萬里收纖雲　一鈎懸碧落
缺圓無定時　人間幾愁樂

78 *Distant Mountain Swept by Clouds*

aimlessly rolling from caves
one wave and the slopes are gone
changing to mist with the turn of a hand
no place for the demon of drought

The first line is from T'ao Yuan-ming's "The Return": "Looking up I gaze into the distance / clouds aimlessly roll out of caves." The second line quotes Huang Keng's "Evening Stroll in the West Garden in Spring": "When the last crimson rays fade / one wave and the mountain is gone." The third line comes from Tu Fu's "Ballad of Poor Friends": "The turn of a hand and there's clouds / another turn and there's rain." And the last line recalls "River of Clouds" in the *Book of Songs:* "The demon of drought is cruel / like fire, like flames."

遥山抹雲

無心出岫時　山腰橫一抹

爲霖覆手間　豈容留旱魃

Fading

Sixteen Branches

79 *Star-lined* Hat

set with stars adorned with jade
glittering lights of morning court
men of rank with heads of snow
Kao and K'uei on the left and right

This particular hat was made of leather triangles sewn together with jewels along the seams. It was worn by senior officials during their dawn audience with the emperor. Among the earliest ministers for which records exist were those who served 4,500 years ago in the court of Emperor Shun. Kao Yao was Shun's minister of justice. K'uei was his minister of music.

會星弁

欲謝一十六枝

星會飾以王 燦燦光朝儀
重臣頭似雪 左右應皐夔

80 *Wine-Straining Bandanna*

falling down drunk is the life for me
kowtowing brings regrets
I'd rather drink with the yellow flowers
a black silk hat isn't worth my time

The yellow flowers of the chrysanthemum are infused in hot water as well as in spirits. It was the favorite flower of the fourth-century poet T'ao Yuan-ming, who was famous for his love of wine as well as his disdain for official position. Chinese officials and members of the gentry were rarely without some sort of head covering. A hat of black silk was customary for officials carrying out their normal duties, while a simple bandanna was worn by peasants or people of modest means.

漉酒巾

爛醉是生涯　折腰良可嘅

欲酒對黄華　烏紗奚足愛

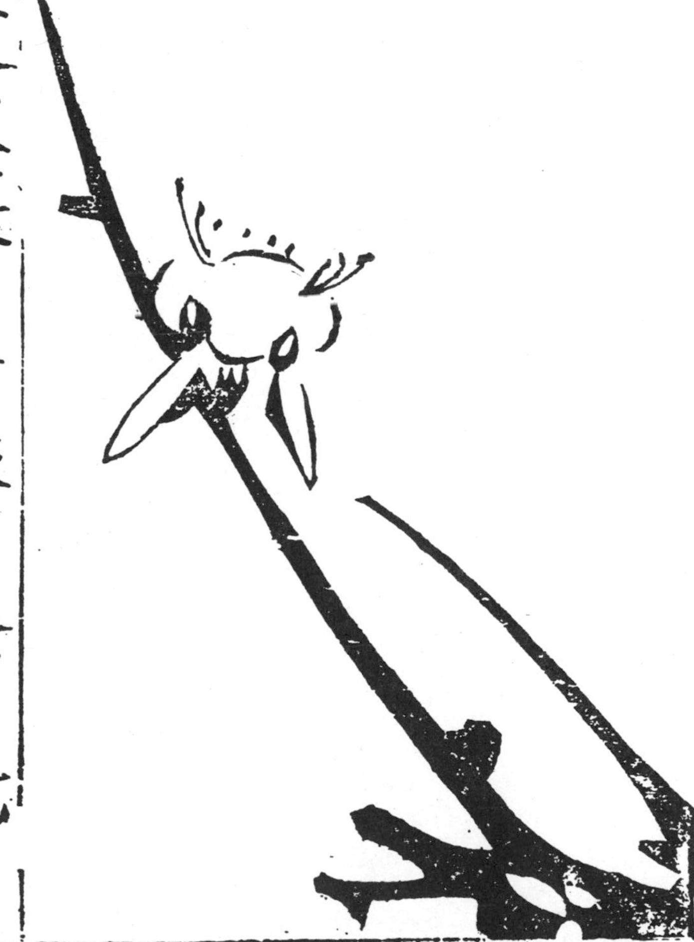

81 *Cicada Clinging to a Leaf*

as willow and locust shade grows dark
the lonely chant grows stronger
among the immortals drinking dew
who says the queen of Ch'i grieves

The willow and the locust are two of the most common shade trees in China. In the third century B.C., the state of Ch'in was able to convince the king of Ch'i not to join a coalition against it. As a result, Ch'in was able to defeat the other states, including Ch'i, and unite all of China under its rule. The king of Ch'i's wife so lamented her husband's blindness to Ch'in's intentions that she died of grief and turned into a cicada. The cicada is an emblem of immortality, and the Chinese often place its jade likeness in the mouths of loved ones prior to burial. Rising out of the earth in spring and shedding its exuviae, it spends its summer afternoons in concert with other cicadas before returning to the earth in fall for another transformation. Dew is the drink of immortals, although wine is a close second.

抱葉蟬

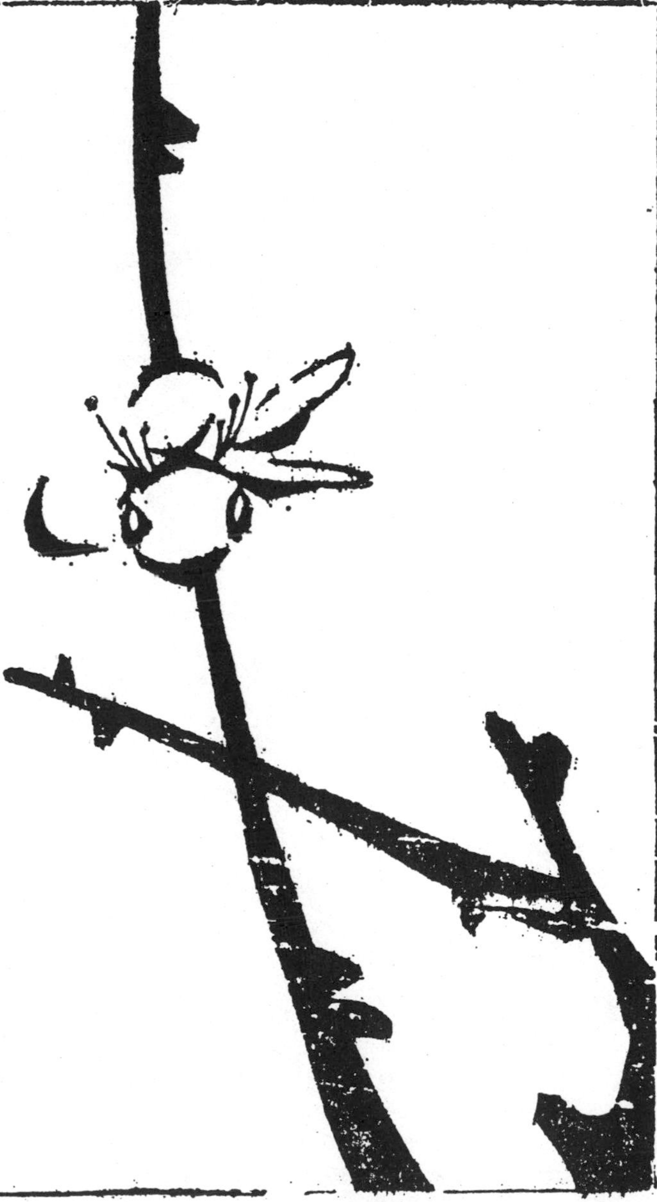

槐柳午陰濃　凄涼聲愈健

飲露已成仙　孰云齊女怨

82 *Butterfly among Flowers*

in the world once he dreamed
the east wind blew in vain
Chuang-tzu soaring free
still loved the charm of flowers

The east wind blows profit and fame. Chuang-tzu relates how he once dreamed he was a butterfly fluttering among flowers. But when he awoke, he didn't know if he had dreamed he was a butterfly, or if he was a butterfly dreaming he was Chuang-tzu (*Chuangtzu,* 2). Here, Sung Po-jen uses flowers ironically to symbolize the illusions and attachments of the contemplative life.

穿花蝶

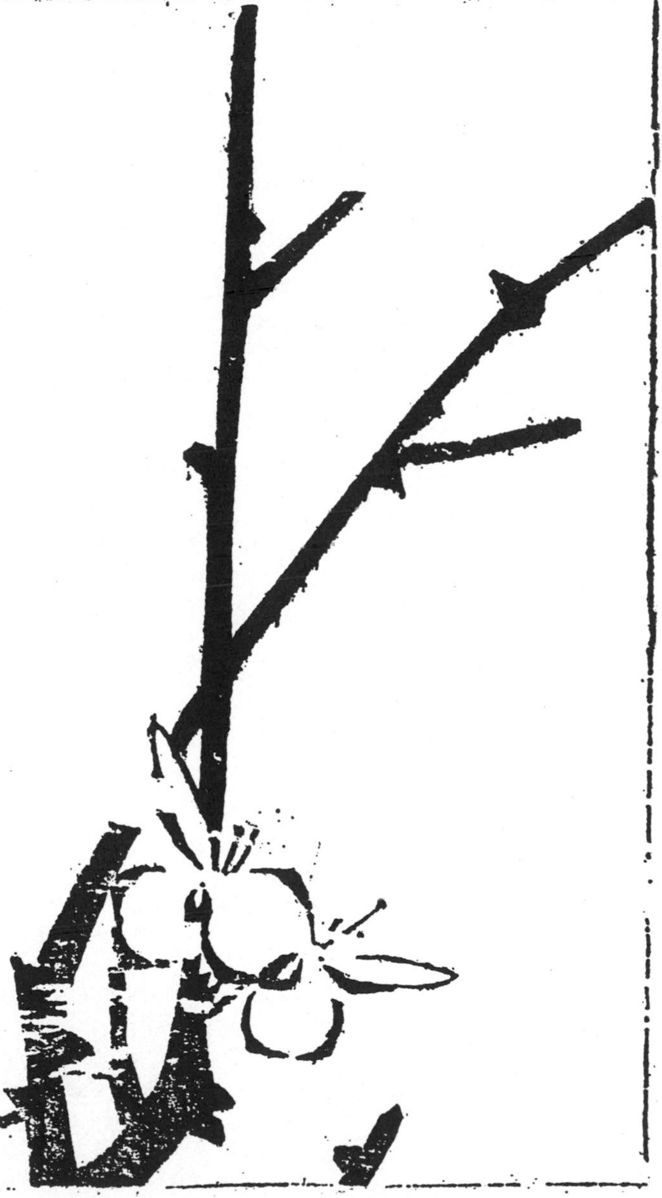

一夢在人間　東風吹不竟
莊周鴻冥冥　胡戀花枝巧

83 *Flying to the Woods at Dusk*

weary wings know the way home
to the woods and sleep
to shoot a roosting bird is heartless
wanton cunning brings no blessing

This recalls two poems of T'ao Yuan-ming: "Returning Birds," which ends: "where's the fowler who would shoot / weary birds must rest"; and "The Return," which includes this couplet: "clouds aimlessly rise from the caves / tired birds know the way home." Of Confucius, it was said that he fished but never used a net, that he hunted but never shot at roosting birds (*Analects,* 7).

暮雀投林

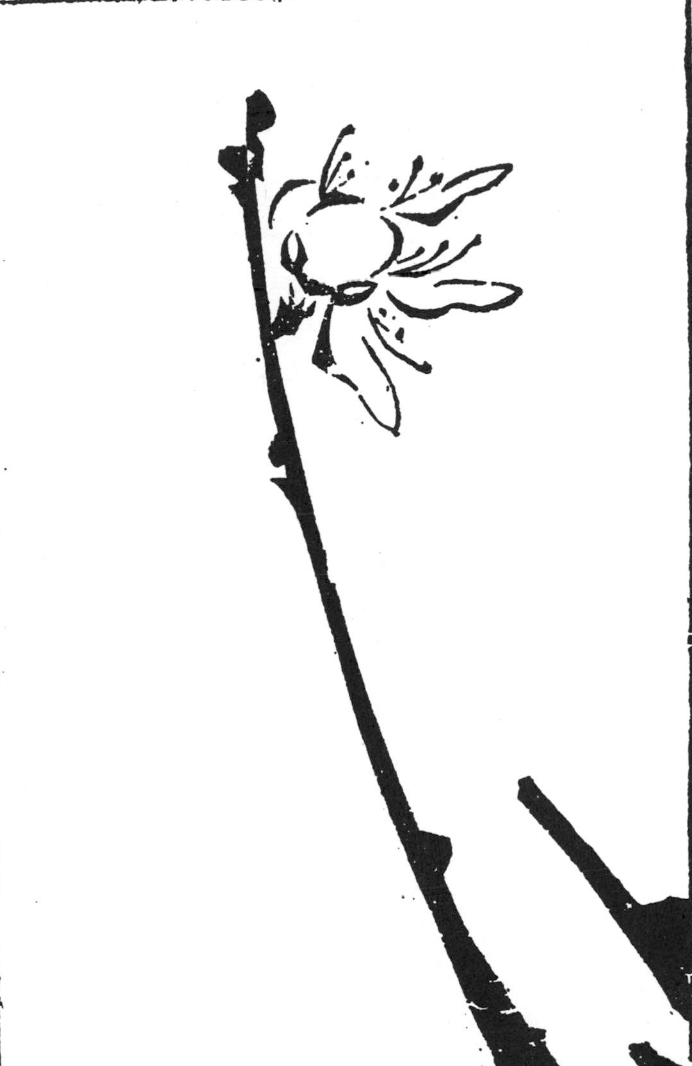

倦翼已知還　投林謀夜宿

弋宿無容心　機深未爲福

84 *Crow Landing on a Tree in Winter*

this applies to men or crows
view a leafless branch with care
the moon is bright why not rest
best to circle three more times

A leafless branch could be a trap. In one of his "Short Ballads," Emperor Wu of the Wei dynasty wrote, "the moon is bright, stars are few / crows and magpies flying south / looking for a branch to rest on / circle trees three times." The crow's care in choosing a branch refers to a gentleman's care in choosing a lord, here represented by the moon.

寒鳥倚樹

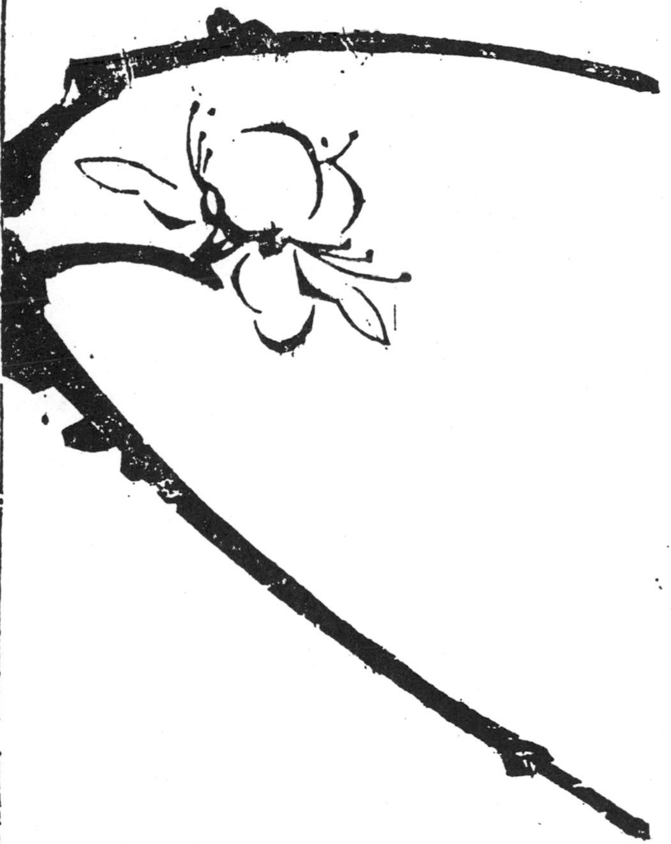

人好鳥亦好　寒枝不輕踏
月明如可依　飛繞猶三匝

85 *Dancer's Sleeves*

longer makes the dancing better
bamboo slips conceal small fingers
when she takes her costume off
we see how short they are

In traditional Chinese dance, long sleeves are swirled like huge ribbons by means of bamboo extensions attached to the dancer's fingers.

舞袖

舞亂更宜長　十笋藏纖指
脫得戲衫時　方知有戲底

86 *Twirling Whiskers*

whiskers whiskers all turned white
the border wind blows cold
king's don't lightly cut their beards
except to restore a general's health

The Chinese esteem beards as signs of long life and consider cutting them to be unlucky as well as unfilial. Once, however, when a T'ang dynasty general became seriously ill, one of the emperor's advisors said he had heard that beard ashes were an effective cure. The emperor was so concerned about his general's health that he cut his own beard to prepare the medicine. Later, when the general recovered and tried to thank him, the emperor said it wasn't for his sake but for the country's.

弄鬚

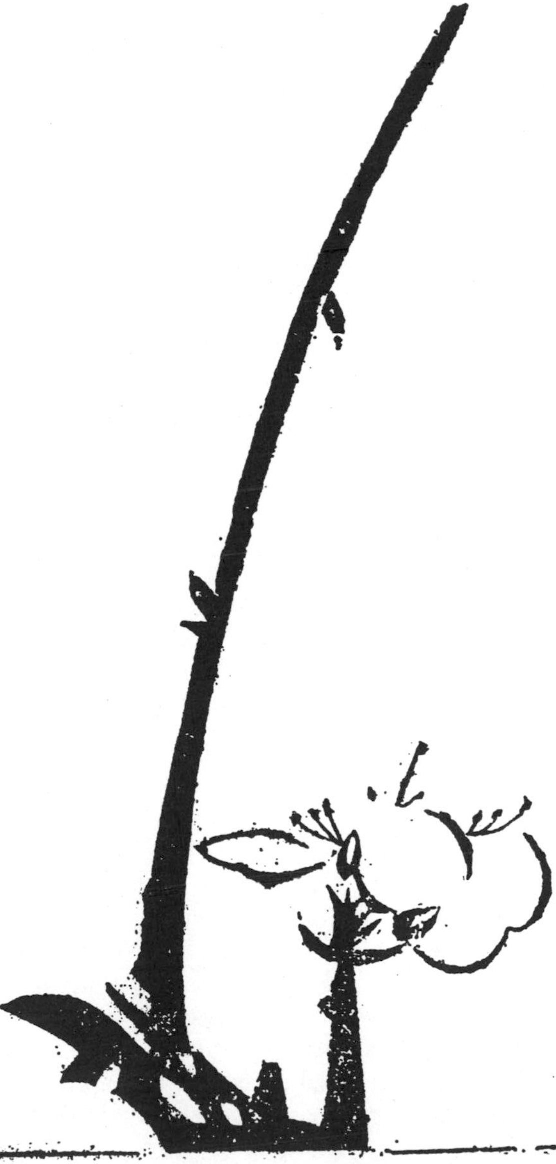

絲絲共白　歷遍風霜寒

君王豈輕剪　欲療將軍安

87 *Oriole Flashing through Willows*

a golden shuttle criss-crosses green silk
the east wind brings clear skies
don't bother singing to find a mate
the green-screen weaver is too tired to weave

The oriole and the willow are both symbols of spring, as is the east wind. Here, the oriole also appears as the golden shuttle and represents a young man in search of his lover, while the green silk window screen, conjured out of hanging willow catkins, refers to the room of an unmarried woman of modest means. The third line is paraphrased from "Cutting Down Trees" in the *Book of Songs,* where birds find mates by singing. And the last line recalls a poem by Pai Chu-yi in which a woman gives up waiting for her lover and stops weaving. Weaving was considered a woman's lifelong duty, unless she never married.

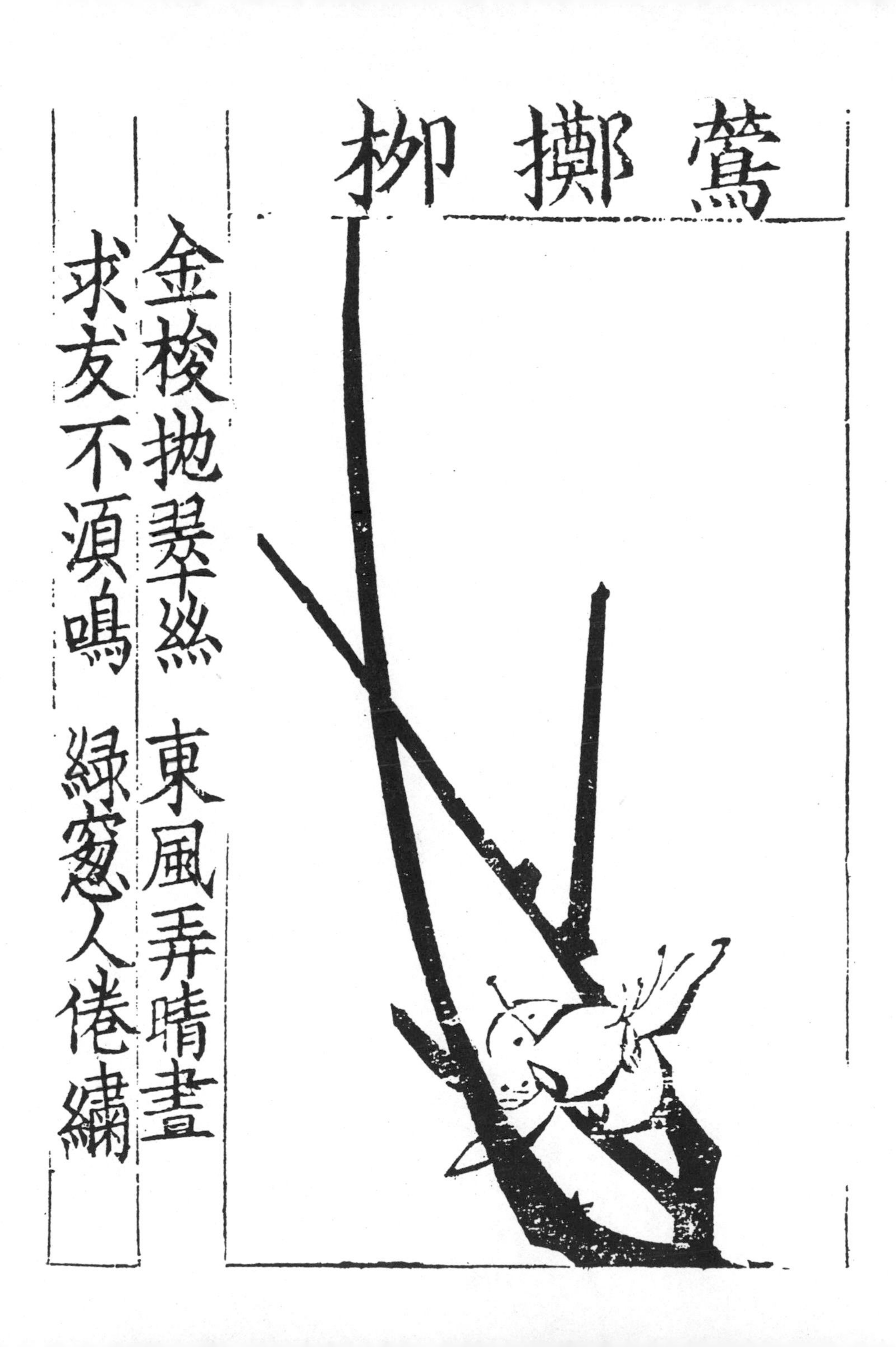

鶯擲柳
金梭抛翠絲　東風弄晴晝
求友不須鳴　緑窻人倦繡

88 *Osprey Riding the Wind*

wings outstretched against the blue
the autumn wind is perfect
pitiful crows and magpies
settle for a branch

In *Chuangtzu,* greater and lesser knowledge are likened to a huge bird whose wings fill the sky and a small bird that makes do with a single branch (Ch. 1).

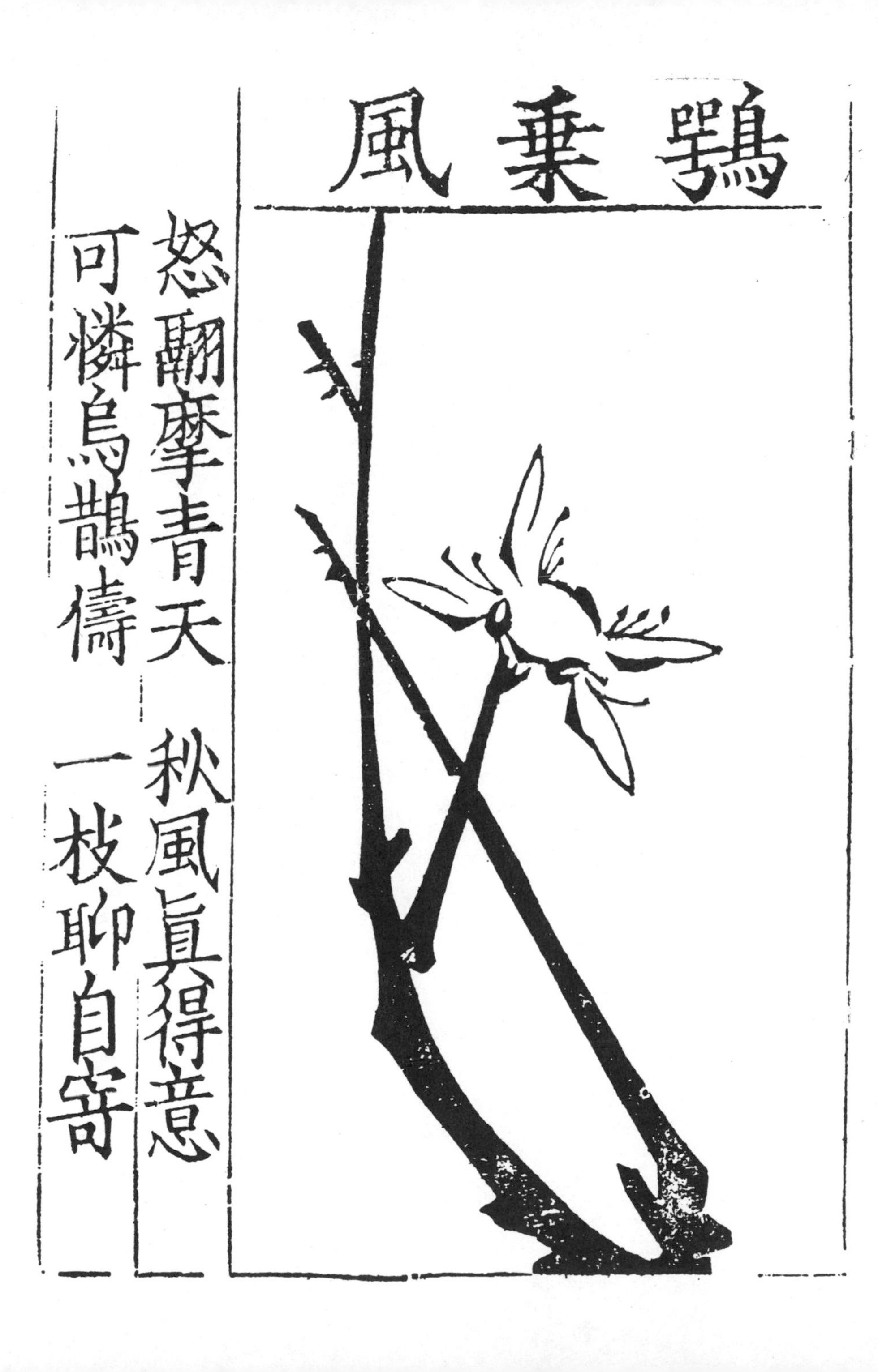
鶻秉風
怒翮摩青天 秋風眞得意
可憐烏鵲儔 一枝聊自寄

89 *Snowcap*

T'ai-liu scatters celestial flowers
a scented branch combats the white
indistinct from finest jade
they call for our cold laughter

T'ai-liu is the snow god, and the petal-like flakes he scatters are said to rival those of the plum in appearance but not in fragrance.

頂雪

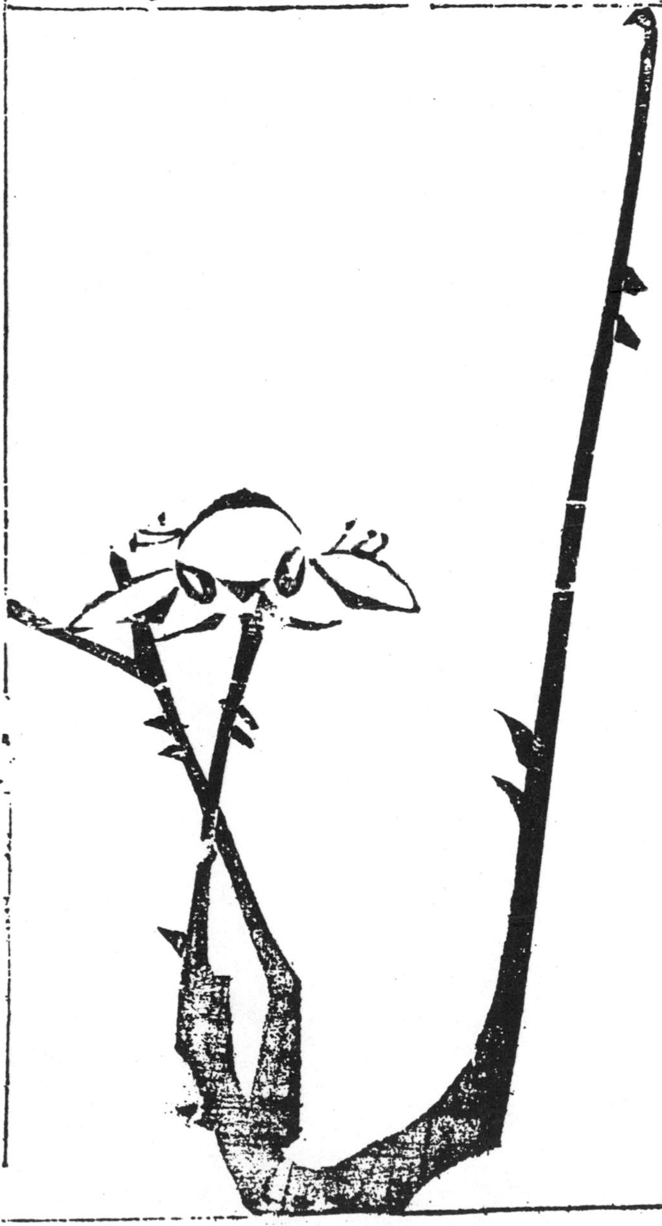

滕六雨天花　南枝香鬬白
瓊玉兩模糊　冷笑從君索

90 *Windblown*

where does the hidden scent come from
wafted by a winter gale
may the Lord of the East protect it
keep it from gracing palace faces

"Hidden scent," is another name for the plum blossom, and recalls Lin Pu's famous couplet written at his hermitage in Hangchou in the eleventh century: "its hidden fragrance rides the wind / the moon shines through the mist." The Lord of the East is the sun, the ruler of spring, at whose distant approach the plum surprises the winter landscape with its bloom. In addition to powder and paint, palace ladies also decorated their faces with flower petals.

欹風

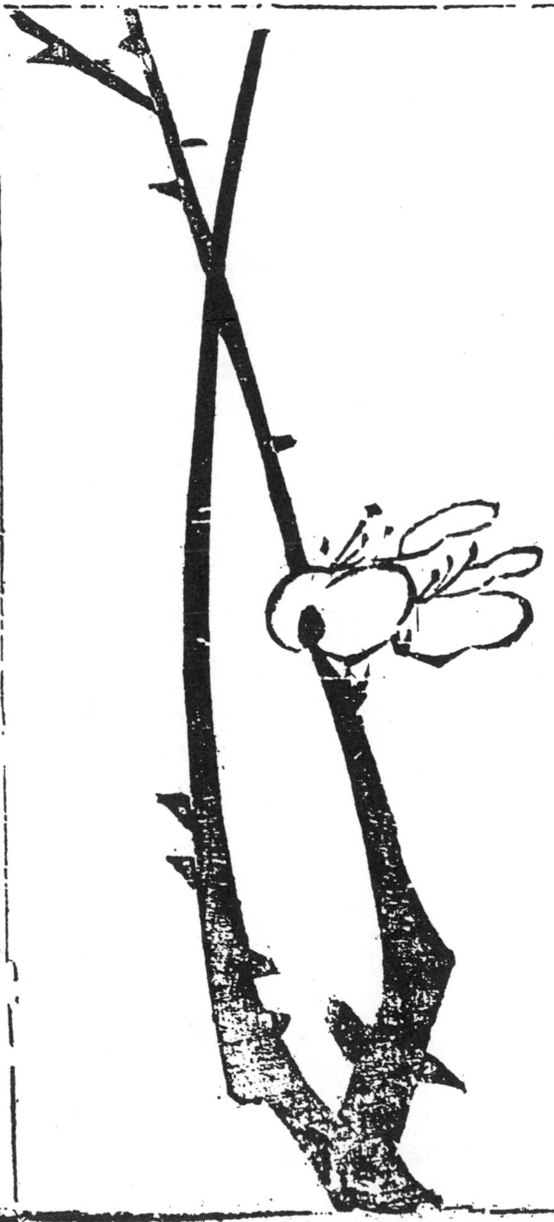

暗香從何來　寒飈爲輕扇
東君須護持　莫點宮粧面

91 *Dragonfly Landing*

four wings of thinnest silk
without a trace of dust
perched upon a silken line
a fisherman's old partner

This poem recalls Tu Fu's "Visiting Again the Ho Family Home," where the dragonfly's license to perch on a fisherman's line refers to the familiarity that comes with a long-standing friendship.

蜻蜓欲立

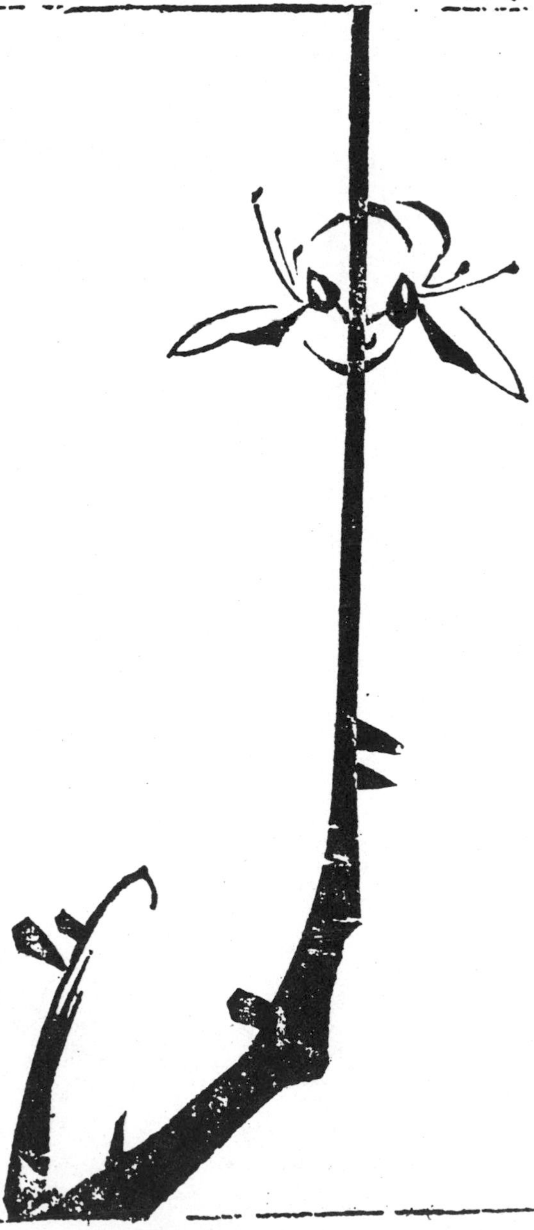

四翼薄於紗　纖塵不相着
只在釣絲邊　漁翁素盟約

92 *Mantis Trying to Fly*

my arms aren't strong enough
and catching insects isn't safe
the cicada's song reveals no fear
high above the oriole watches

Among Chuang-tzu's many stories is one in which he uses the example of a mantis trying to stop a cart to represent a person's unrealistic assessment of his abilities (*Chuangtzu*, 4). Another writer sees a mantis preparing to grab a cicada and is reminded of a king who rushes to attack a neighboring state without bothering about the consequences. The cicada, it turns out, is about to be grabbed by an oriole, and the oriole is about to be shot by one of the king's advisors (*Shuoyuan*, 9).

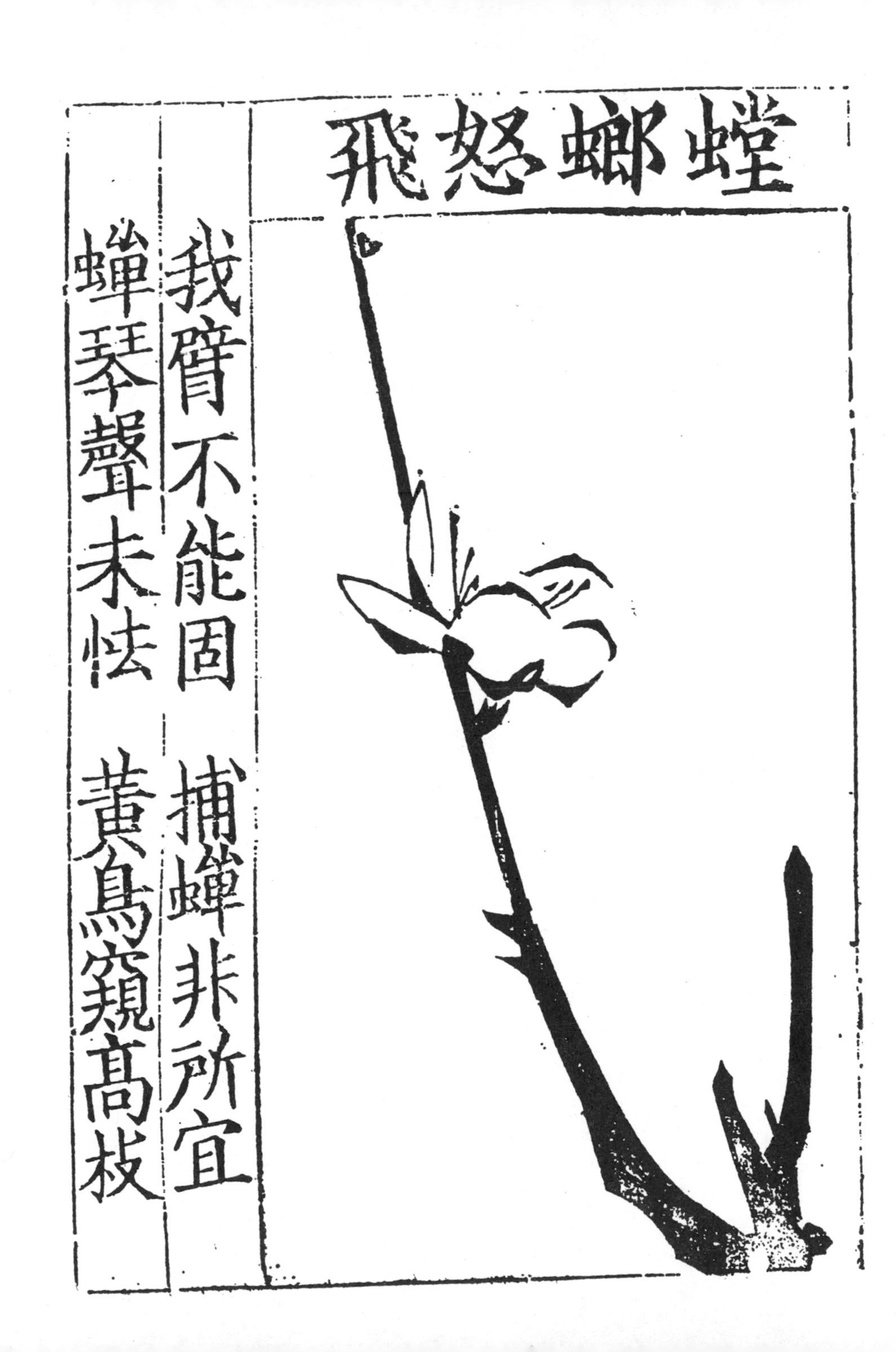
螳螂怒飛
我臂不能固 捕蟬非所宜
蟬琴聲未怯 黃鳥窺高枝

93 *Magpie Rocking on a Branch*

in the sky where two stars meet
a bridge spans Silver River
another year since they parted
twitter twitter idle news

According to an ancient Chinese legend, the Sun married his daughter, Vega, to the Herdboy Star, Altair, in hopes that she would find an interest in life other than weaving. Unfortunately, his daughter become so enamored of her new lover, she gave up weaving altogether. The Sun was so furious, he ordered the couple to live on opposite shores of the Silver River, or Milky Way, except for one night a year, the seventh night of the seventh moon. On this night, magpies form a bridge on which the two lovers meet. The Chinese still celebrate this as Lover's Night.

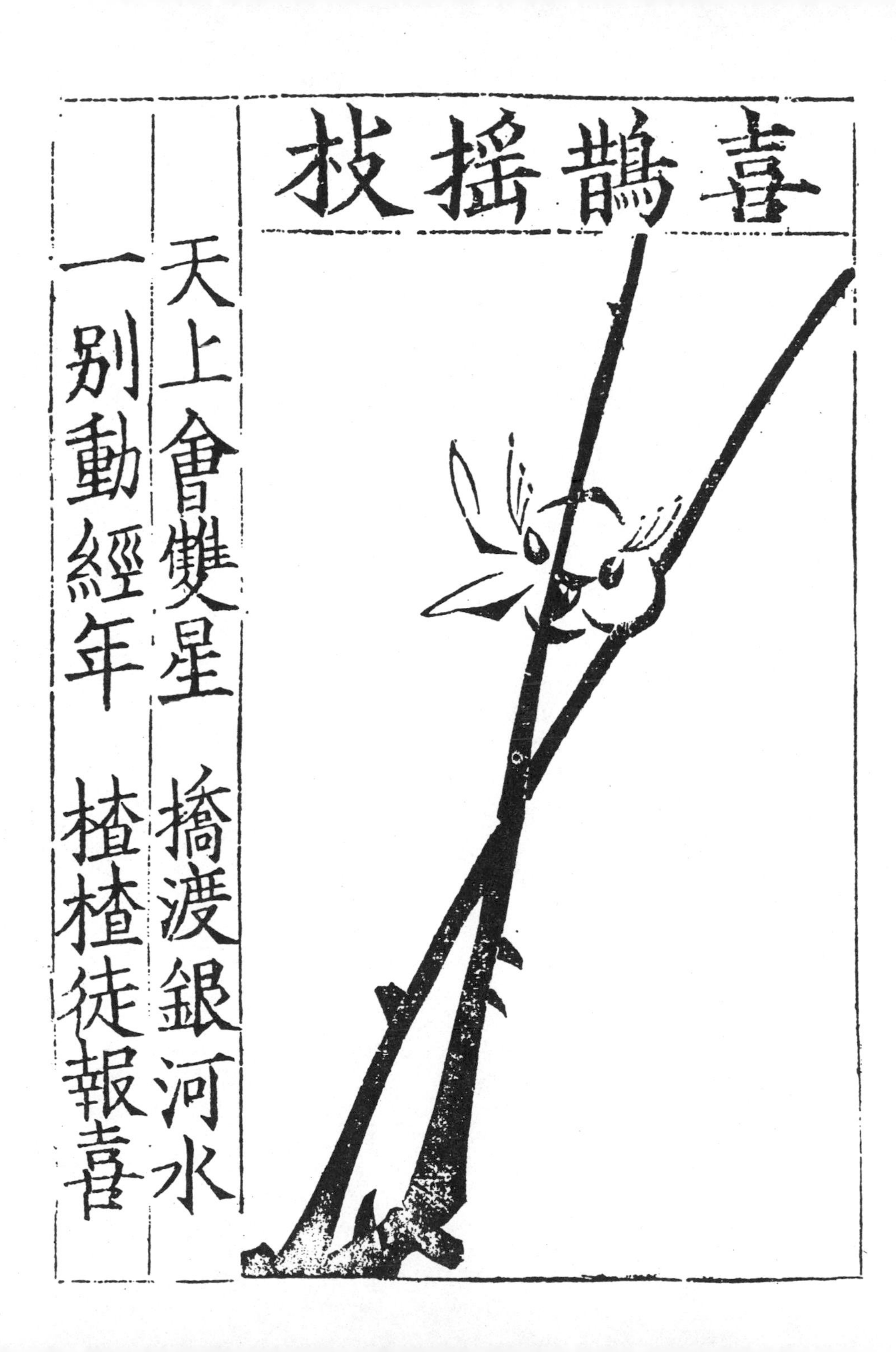
喜鵲搖枝
天上會雙星
橋渡銀河水
一別動經年
楂楂徒報喜

94 *Fish Spitting Water*

spring skies are clear and waves are bright
vagabond soul of rivers and lakes
a perfect thirty-six scales
leap through Yu Gate in one try

The Yellow River is famous for its carp, which the Chinese also call "thirty-six scales" after a series of thirty-six black scales along the fish's flank. Yumen, or Yu Gate, is an opening in the middle reaches of the Yellow River named after Yu the Great, who built his capital nearby in Linfen and who first brought the flooding of the Yellow River under control 4,200 years ago. When the Yellow River's water level recedes in winter, rapids appear at Yu Gate, and carp work their way with difficulty to their ancient spawning grounds upstream. The chance of passing the civil service exams and gaining an official appointment was likened to a carp's getting through this section of the river.

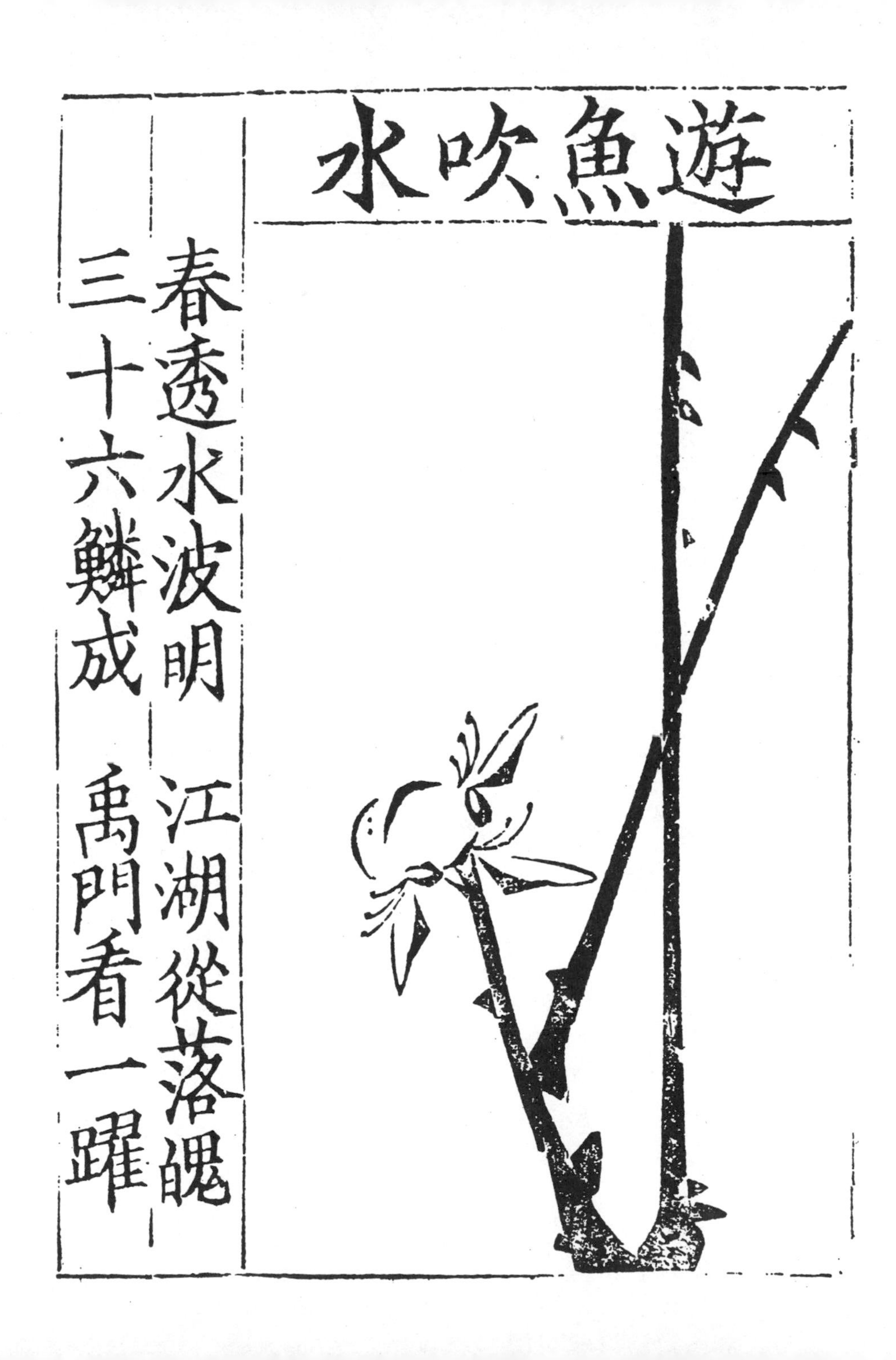

遊魚吹水
春透水波明
江湖從落魄
三十六鱗成
禹門看一躍

Forming Fruit

Six Branches

95 *Four Worthies of Chungnan*

lending wings to the House of Han
in the world yet free from form
there's true joy right here
not only on Mount Shang

At the end of the third century B.C., four white-haired men of integrity refused to serve the oppressive First Emperor of the Ch'in dynasty and retired to Mount Shang on the southern slopes of the Chungnan Mountains. After the Han dynasty replaced the Ch'in, Emperor Kao-tsu was on the point of replacing the crown prince, when the four sages left the mountains and came to the boy's aid.

The 1261 edition mistakenly titles this section "Four Branches" instead of "Six." I've corrected it in English.

橘中四皓

就實四枝

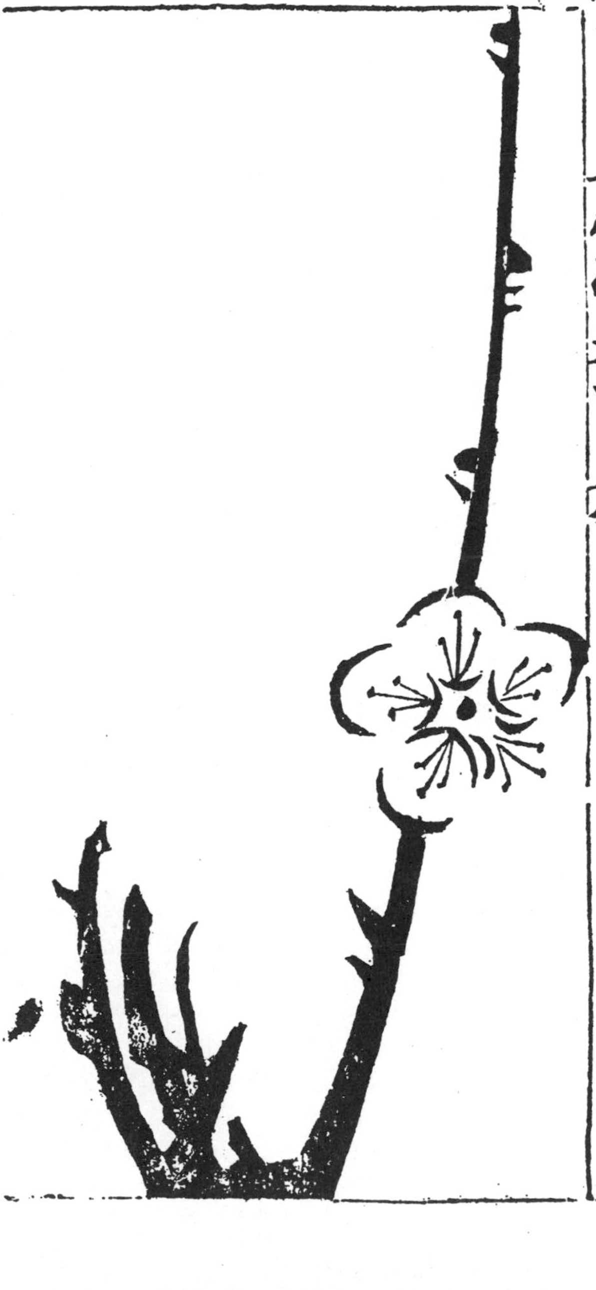

羽翼漢家了　志形天地間
箇中有眞樂　奚必拘商山

96 *Three High-minded Men of Wuchiang*

p'in looks like three floating tubs
it means an end to Wuchiang snow
remember the red smartweed flower
don't talk about profit or fame

Wuchiang was a name for the area along the Yangtze near the borders of the modern provinces of Kiangsu and Chekiang. Three men who became recluses in this region included Fan Li in the fifth century B.C., Chang Han in the fourth century A.D., and Lu Kuei-meng in the eighth century. All three placed great emphasis on personal integrity, which is among the meanings of *p'in.* Sung Po-jen sees the three mouths that make up the character *p'in* floating along as the sort of tubs people still sit in while gathering edible plants that grow in China's waterways and marshlands in summer. Among marsh plants, smartweed is distinguished by its sprays of rust-colored, three-petalled flowers. Although edible, its bitter flavor and wild habitat has led to its association with hardship.

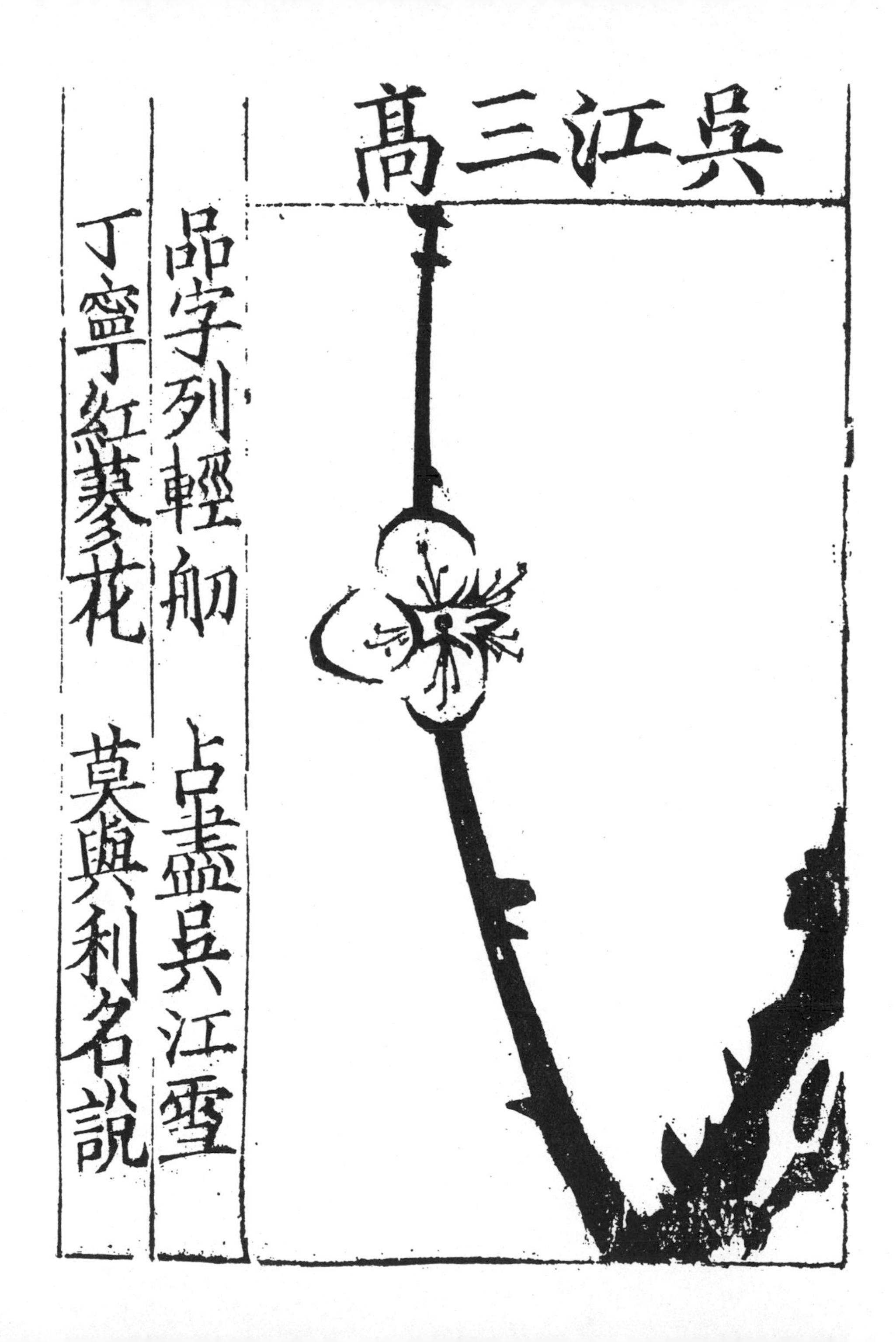
吳江三高
品字列輕舠
占盡吳江雪
丁寧紅蓼花
莫與利名說

97 *Two Shu's*

East Gate wind blows lightly
two pendants pure as water
why did those who saw them off
not know enough to leave

Shu Kuang and his nephew Shu Shou served as senior and junior tutors to the crown prince during the reign of Emperor Hsuan in the first century A.D. After the crown prince ascended the throne as Emperor Yuan, they decided to retire to the countryside with their reputations intact, here represented by the simple, pure white pendants they wore at their waists. Such was the esteem in which they were held, all the officials in Ch'ang-an came to see them off outside the capital's East Gate. Many Chinese historians have viewed the reign of Emperor Yuan as the beginning of the Han dynasty's decline.

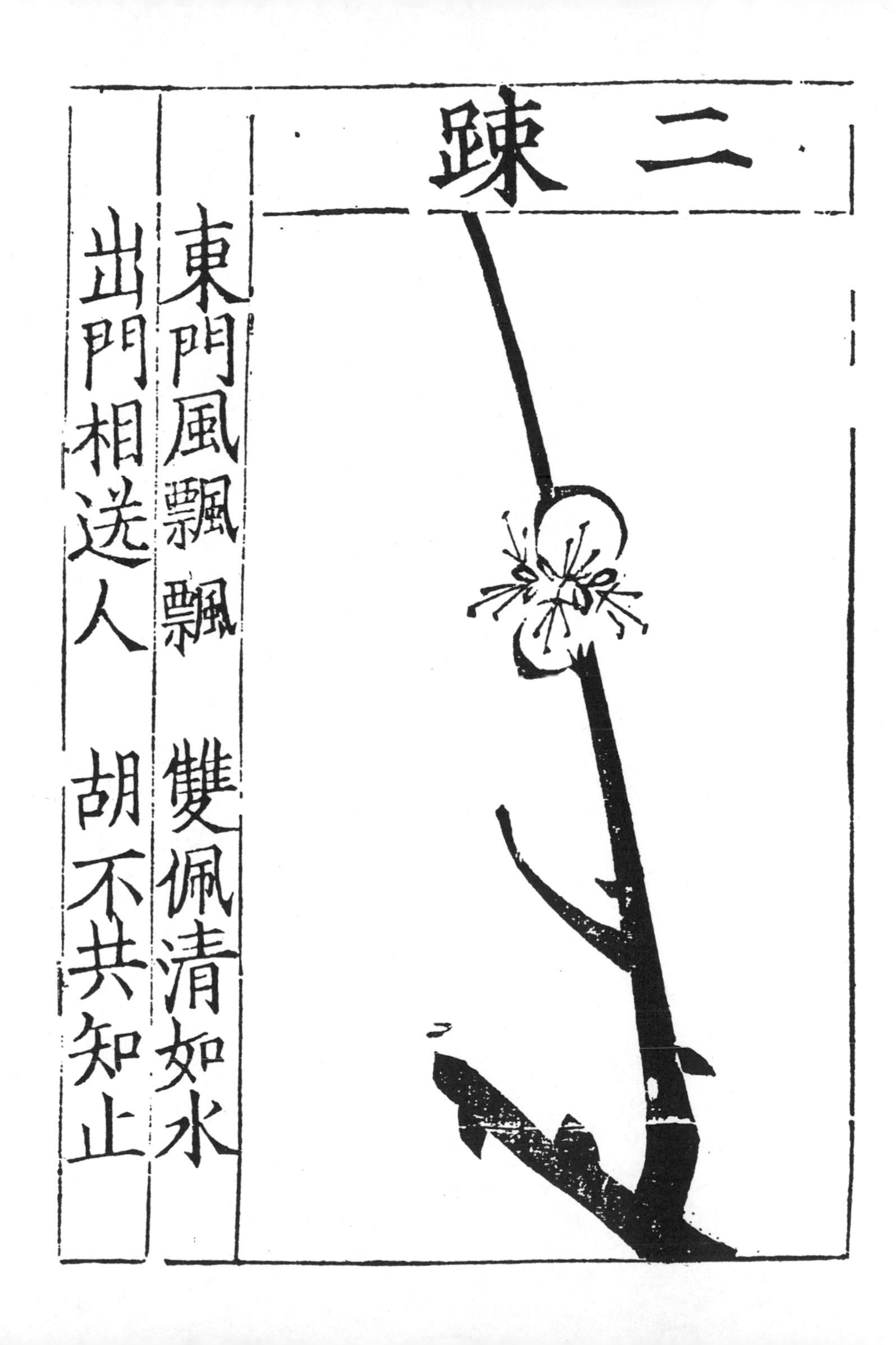
二踈
東門風飄飄　雙佩清如水
出門相送人　胡不共知止

98 *Fishing Alone*

his pole alone in the cold and rain
living apart at Yenling Bend
sleeping with his feet stretched out
he showed us Kuang-wu's stature

Yen Tzu-ling, who lived in the first century A.D., spent his days fishing from a rock that still bears his name along an especially scenic stretch of the Fuchun River south of Hangchou. He was once visited here by his boyhood companion who had since restored the Han dynasty and ascended the throne as Emperor Kuang-wu. Unimpressed with his friend's attainments, Yen Tzu-ling stretched out and fell asleep with his feet on the emperor's stomach. The incident did much to immortalize Kuang-wu as a tolerant ruler.

獨釣

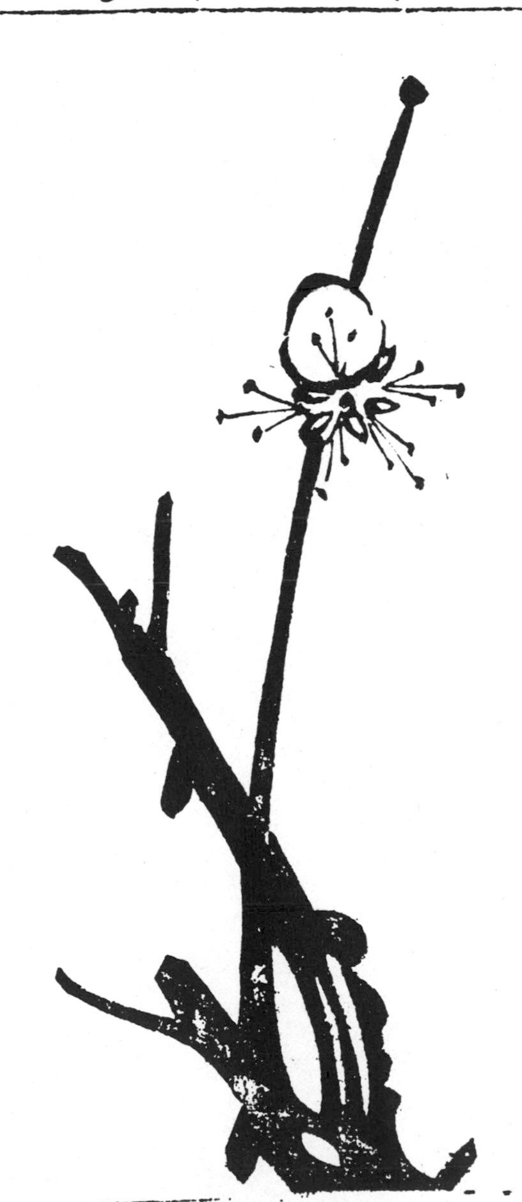

一竿風雨寒　獨占嚴陵瀨

苟非伸脚眠　曷見光武大

99 *Meng Chia's* Falling *Cap*

this drunk's cap doesn't lightly fall
the autumn mums are lovely
how pathetic among the guests
the host can't pick him out

Meng Chia, who lived in the fourth century A.D., was once drinking with a group of officials on the night chrysanthemums are celebrated when his cap blew off. The host noticed that Meng continued drinking as if nothing had happened. When Meng left to relieve himself, the host asked one of his servants to pick up Meng's cap and return it to his seat, and he asked a poet present to compose a poem making fun of the cap. When Meng returned and found his cap and a poem waiting for him, he replied with a poem of his own that earned him universal acclaim. About ten years earlier, a famous judge of men had been able to pick Meng out from a crowd of officials based purely on his reputation. The second line is borrowed from one of T'ao Yuan-ming's *Drinking Poems,* which was inspired by a line by Ch'u Yuan, China's first great poet, about eating the fallen petals of the chrysanthemum. The last two lines also refer to the failure of earlier rulers to recognize the talents of Ch'u and T'ao.

孟嘉落帽

醉帽不輕飛　秋菊有佳色

自慚群座中　主人猶未識

100 *Of Tripods and Soup*

white replaced by blue-green jade
a flavor truly sour
all too soon it's like a dream
the soup is done the world at peace

The Chinese tripod that played such an important role in court rituals was first used as a cooking pot. The sour green fruit that replaces the plum tree's white blossoms is also used as a condiment in cooking. Presenting metaphors for good government, the *Book of Documents* says, "In cooking soup, be my salt and plums." (4.8)

商鼎催羹

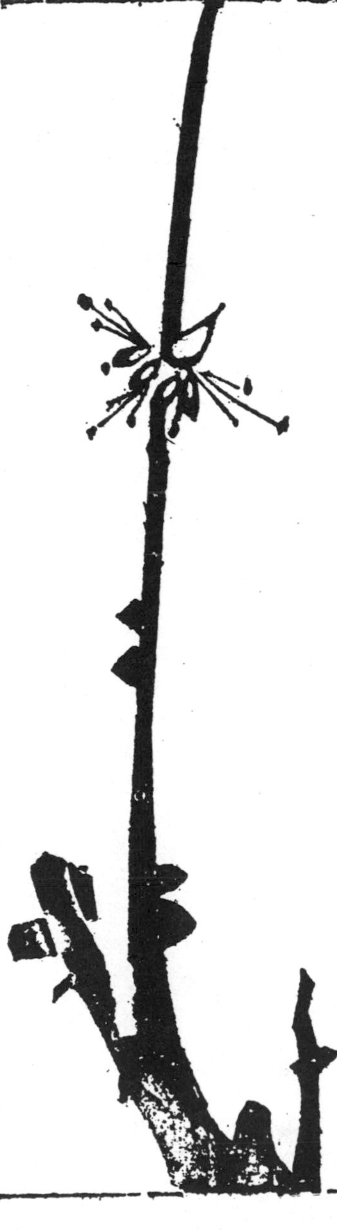

脫白弄青玉　風味猶辛酸

指日夢惟肖　羹調天下安

卷終

SUNG PO-JEN was a Chinese poet of the thirteenth century. RED PINE, who also writes under the name BILL PORTER, is the author of *Road to Heaven: Encounters with Chinese Hermits,* as well as the translator of *The Zen Teaching of Bodhidharma.* LO CH'ING is Executive Secretary of Chinese PEN and an advisor to Taiwan's Ministry of Culture.

A note on the spelling of Chinese names: A modified Wade-Giles system, in which umlauts have been omitted, is used throughout. Exceptions include book and place names, where the hyphens and apostrophes have been removed and the words run together (Chuangtzu instead of Chuang-tzu, Tungting instead of Tung-t'ing), and names for which a prior usage has been established (Sian instead of Hsi-an, Yangtze instead of Ch'ang-chiang).